JUSTIFICATION
An Ecumenical Study

JUSTIFICATION
An Ecumenical Study

George H. Tavard

PAULIST PRESS
New York/Ramsey

Library of Congress
Catalog Card Number: 83-60374

ISBN: 0-8091-2549-8

Published by Paulist Press
545 Island Road, Ramsey, N.J. 07446

Printed and bound in the
United States of America

CONTENTS

FOREWORD

Ever since October 31, 1517, when he presented ninety-five theses for disputation, Martin Luther has been a question mark for Catholic theology. Few Catholics of those who have read him carefully have been satisfied with the condemnation which Pope Leo X fulminated against him in 1520. The violence of the polemics in which Luther was involved with the defenders of the papacy tended in fact to becloud the basic issues. In many cases political motivations and purposes among his princely supporters or adversaries made it impossible to discuss his fundamental options with detachment. As disagreement emerged within the ranks of the reformers, many side-issues obscured the central problem. Furthermore the channels followed by the theology of the Counter-Reformation left the questions asked by Luther largely unanswered. There lay toward the limits of the horizon of Catholic theology a *terra incognita* in which few cared to venture: this was the theology of Martin Luther.

Only recently have some Catholic theologians taken a new look at the issues raised by the German friar of the sixteenth century. Still more recently suggestions have been made toward bridging the gap between the doctrine of Luther and the official formulation of Roman Catholic teaching. Especially in German-speaking countries, Catholic historical scholarship has largely rehabilitated Luther. Official dialogues between the Lutheran and the Roman Catholic traditions, which began in the United States in 1965, have, in several joint statements, narrowed the differences between the two sides in such matters as eucharistic theology and the ministry, and even in the more emotional questions of the primacy and infallibility of the bishop of Rome. Yet one may still wonder if the basic problems of the material and the formal aspects of the Reformation—Scripture alone and justification by faith—have now been solved.

1

In 1959 I examined the first of these points in a major study, *Holy Writ or Holy Church. The Crisis of the Protestant Reformation.* The controversies over Scripture and its interpretation resulted from a misunderstanding that could have been easily cleared up. At the official level, the Constitution *Dei Verbum* of Vatican Council II has gone a long way toward reconciliation on this point.

The second problem—justification by faith—is still of ecumenical importance. As long as no agreement has been attempted on justification, the recent ecumenical dialogues on other controversial topics remain interesting theoretical exercises which need not entail practical action. Examination, at least, and agreement, if possible, as to the heart of the Reformation problematic are called for at the exact point where the cost of reconciliation has so far seemed to be repudiation of the Reformation by the followers of the reformers. For to reject justification by faith means renouncing the Reformation.

I therefore present this short volume as a study of justification by faith. But both the topic and the circumstances have required another approach than in the case of *Scriptura sola*. Justification raises both a theoretical question and a practical problem. Theoretically, how can one pass from sin to grace, from alienation from God to friendship with God? Practically, how does one come to believe and accept the Christian faith and norms of behavior? The very meaning of the Christian community is at stake in these questions, and thereby the meaning of all Christian life. Yet such questions are not easily answered or even approached. On the one hand, the experience of being justified by God has been going on for centuries and is still patent in our day. But it appears to be closely linked with the broader experience of conversion. And conversion is many-sided. People have been converted to all sorts of beliefs and ways of life. On the other hand, the basis of Christian conversion in the doctrine of justification relates its structure to the experience of grace. Christian conversion falls within the scope of history; it may be studied phenomenologically. Yet it can be fruitfully studied only in constant reference to theological principles. These two ways of approach should be complementary, the historical and personal event of conversion being normally explained by theological and spiritual principles relating to justification.

The basic problem appears to be simple. To show this I will attempt to define three terms:

- *Conversion* is the exchange of one set of beliefs for another.
- *Justification* is the event of becoming just, of passing from a state of sin to a state of basic holiness.
- *Sanctification* is the manifestation and development of this basic holiness in all aspects of life.

The basic problem regards the exact relationships of these three events. Is justification brought about by conversion? Is sanctification necessary to the fullness of justification? A responsible theological treatment of these questions should both start from Scripture and take account of the state of the question before the Reformation. This in turn demands examination of patristic and medieval theology. But each of these three areas of research—Scripture, the Fathers, the Middle Ages—has been and could still be the object of extensive study. Material has therefore to be selected and a methodology adopted which, by the same token, will exclude other material and methods. Exhaustiveness of documentation would be self-defeating. One must opt for a practical criterion: to select enough material to throw light on the basic aspects of the problem; to find a method which works. In the method I have adopted, I have placed Luther at the center, simply because his formulation of the doctrine of justification contained an implicit (at times explicit) critique of all previous formulas and became a point of contention after him. In treating Luther, I have also had to be selective. I have chiefly studied two of his basic works, the *Commentary on Galatians* of 1519, and the better known *Commentary on Galatians* of 1535. An early and a later work on the same subject have the advantage of letting shine both the constant elements and the developments of an author's thoughts (Chapter III).

This is preceded by a more cursory study of justification in the New Testament. But I have adopted for this an unconventional method. The doctrine is essentially that of Paul in his great Epistles. As there would be little point in writing a summary of the abundant material which exists on Paul, I have adopted a special angle, the doctrine of justification as reflected in Luke's accounts of the conversion

of Paul (Chapter I). This is followed by a survey of patristic and medieval conceptions, the theology of Augustine forming a major stepping-
stone between Paul and Luther (Chapter II). My presentation of
Luther is followed by a survey of justification after the Reformation.
On the Catholic side, I have surveyed the teaching of the Council of
Trent and its sequel, including the First Vatican Council. On the Protestant side, I have examined what has been the major departure from
Luther's theology, namely John Wesley's doctrine on Christian perfection, ending this chapter with John Henry Newman's typology of
justification theories (Chapter IV). Finally, I have presented some
reassessments of Luther's central doctrine by recent Catholic theologians, especially as this doctrine is epitomized in the phrase, *simul
justus et peccator* (Chapter V), thus bringing this book to an ecumen-
ically-oriented conclusion. The part of Chapter III dealing with the
Commentary on Galatians of 1519 and a first version of Chapter V
were presented for discussions at two meetings of "Lutherans and
Catholics in Dialogue."

I.

THE WITNESS OF THE NEW TESTAMENT

The teaching of the New Testament on the nature of justification has been the subject of wide disagreements. This is hardly surprising, since the same canon of Scripture contains Paul's Epistles to the Galatians and the Romans, which speak of justification by faith, and the Epistle of James, which speaks of justification by works. Thus there are obvious differences in the text, interpretation of which has never been easy. To these, exegetes and theologians, to say nothing of preachers, have added doctrinal and other divergences which they have brought to their approach of the text. If all are agreed on the principle that justification of the unjust is the work of God in or through Jesus the Christ—because this is what identifies the Christian faith—the doctrinal unanimity on justification ends here. Is justification also the result, in part, of one's own efforts? Is it somehow a reward for a previously good life? Is it brought about by obedience to the commandments? By prayer and good works? By repentance? Is it a pure gift? Or is it to be worked out for oneself in fear and trembling? The list of possible questions to which Christians would give different answers would be a long one.

Some of the theological disagreements which have emerged in the Church's history will be reviewed in the later chapters of this book. In this first chapter I intend to look at what one can gather to be the central message of the New Testament on the question. My concern is not to survey older or recent New Testament scholarship, a task which has already been done better than I could do it. Nor is it to bring everyone to agree on all the details of a doctrine on justification.

It is to attempt to find a vantage point which may enable us to perceive the main focus of the New Testament doctrine or doctrines on the question.

This search must have something to do with Paul's understanding of the Gospel. I believe that all contemporary theologians would agree to this, even those who wish to balance the teaching of Paul with that of other witnesses, such as the authors of the four Gospels, or the writers of the Petrine Epistles, or James, or the Johannine literature as a whole. There have indeed been many studies on Paul.[1] Yet, here again, no consensus on the proper methodology has been arrived at. Certainly, the meaning of terms relating to justice, as used by Paul and others, is relevant. The main ones are *dikaioo* (to make just), *dikaiosynè* (righteousness), *dikaios* (innocent, just), and *dikaioma* (justice, righteousness). But other terms may also be important, especially those which relate to sin, forgiveness, repentance, atonement, expiation, and conversion, as well as salvation, redemption, and reconciliation. And the problem is not only of determining the meaning of terms. It is also of determining the purpose of parables and techniques, the implications of events and actions, and, not least, the relationships of all these to the person and career of Jesus, whose name, Jeshouah, precisely means Savior.

None of the questions implied in such an extensive field of research can be fully answered unless one takes account of the Old Testament background. Here, the covenant between God and Israel is effective of whatever righteousness may be claimed for the people of God. The testimony of the prophets often had to do with the true understanding of *hesed* (justice). The determination of their message requires examining how *hesed* relates to *ahabah* (love), especially if it is true that the New Testament word for love, *agapē,* is a transliteration of the Hebrew word.[2] The great school of thought of the Pharisees, which dominated Israel at the time of Jesus, was primarily involved in the question: How can the children of Abraham be right (just) in the eyes of God and of neighbor? One may gather from the letters of Paul that part of the polemics between the early churches and the synagogues turned around the question of true righteousness and how to obtain it. But here also I see no need to duplicate, imitate, or summarize the many studies which are already extant.

I have therefore severely restricted both the method and the scope of the present chapter, at the risk of seeming to be arbitrary to some. Rather than justify my choice *a priori,* however, I would suggest that, as the proof of the pudding is in the eating, so the worth of a method appears from the trying.

The method I have adopted will seem unusual to many. It draws on structuralism. Structural methods are already well known in some theological circles and have been applied to the study of the New Testament. Yet they have not yet been widely accepted or even tried as a way of approach to the biblical text.[3] To explain it briefly, the method presupposes that a written text, like a spoken discourse, covers an underlying structure, which is to it what a frame is to a building. But unlike the frame of a house, which is necessarily known to the architect and the builder, the structure of a text is not necessarily known to the author. To those who are able to determine what the structure is, however, the latent intentions of the author appear in plain view, even regardless of the teaching, if any, which the author intentionally included in the text. Undoubtedly, such a research of basic structure cannot replace historical, philological, exegetical, and other literary analyses which attempt to discover the author's intention, purpose, or meaning. But it can bring support to, or reveal, convergences with the conclusions of more classical methods. In some cases, it can even open a short-cut to the real meaning of a text, for once a text is written, it stands by itself apart from its writer; it has its meaning or meanings regardless of what its author would have understood in it. My chosen methodology will of course be more understandable to those who are familiar with my volume on the relation of structural method to the work of theologizing.

I have elected to make a structural analysis relating to Paul's conception of justification. But rather than study the famous passages of Galatians and Romans, I have selected Luke's account of Paul's conversion as a basic test case. I am well aware of historians' objections that there are no less than three such accounts in Acts, that their discrepancies throw doubt on their accuracy, that each may be entirely reconstructed by Luke himself in line with his conception of a historian's task, and that they betray Luke's doctrine rather than Paul's. However, one can also argue that justification, the rendering just of the sinner, can be properly envisaged as pinpointing what constitutes the heart of the fundamental Christian experience of conversion. And there is a sense in which Paul's conversion must be, in the New Testament, paradigmatic. If the early Church found the source of its faith in the remembrance of Jesus and in the experience of his continuing presence and guidance, it could not find in him a suitable model for conversion. Indeed, the modern practice of presenting something called "the faith of Jesus" to imitation and emulation has no equivalent in the New Testament.[4] Whatever original experience may have been at the start of Jesus' human self-awareness and religious consciousness was not recorded in the Gospels, even though the accounts of Jesus' baptism by John may hint at some lines of thought. Paul's life, however, clearly hinged around a basic conversion experience. This, more than anything else in the writings of the New Testament, could be taken as the very type and norm of justification as constituting the heart of conversion.

Paul mentions his conversion in Galatians 1:12–17 and may allude to it in 1 Corinthians 9:1 and 15:8. Details, however, are given only by Luke at three places in Acts (9:3–9; 22:6–10; 26:9–12).[5] I will call these three versions I, II, and III. There is admittedly no way of sorting out what is strict historical record and what is Luke's rhetorical reconstruction. Yet the problem is not to know what happened in a historical time sequence. It is to understand how Paul saw himself as having passed from injustice (being unjust in God's eyes) to justice (being just in God's eyes).

In all three accounts, the event happens while Saul is on a journey to Damascus. Saul is traveling on a persecuting mission. Ironically, what he is pursuing "till death" is "this way" (22:4); he is after the men and women "of the way" (9:2); he is on the way after "the way."[6] Yet as he "comes" to the city, blind and led by his companions, he has become a changed man. He arrives as one who seeks and is prepared to learn. From one angle, this could be viewed as a fairly ordinary account of a mythical journey in which, through an extraordinary encounter, a reversal of values has taken place. Saul is changed, and so is his world. Jerusalem, the city of the Jewish faith, and Damascus, a city of paganism, interchange their roles, Damascus becoming the city of faith for Saul, who has journeyed from the city of persecution, Jerusalem.[7] The event which has cut his journey in two parts is itself appropriate to a reversal of values: the proud man who thought he knew the truth is blinded; light throws him into darkness; light comes from heaven, and he falls on the earth; the leader needs to be led; having been taken to the city, he is symbolically dead, "sightless, neither eating nor drinking" for three days (9:9). He will return to sight and to life through the mediation of one who stands in interesting contrast with Saul. Ananias, an otherwise unknown disciple, is well versed in the Law and has a good name among the Jews of Damascus (22:12): the un-Christian Judaism of Saul is transformed through the Christian Judaism of Ananias.

The context of the myth[8] is made of multiple contrasts: between Jerusalem and Damascus in their interchanging roles as cities of good and of evil; between the departure of a leader on horseback and the arrival of a groping blind man; between light and darkness; between heaven and earth; between two styles of Judaism; between the journey and "the way." Saul's co-persecutors, who traveled with him toward what turned out to be his blinding, ended up as his guide toward the overcoming of his blindness in Damascus. But while he is the subject of the central event, they remain uncomprehending witnesses, equally blind to the light from heaven and to the night of Saul's blindness. Their status as witnesses is self-contradictory: either they hear but see nothing (9:7), or they see the light but hear nothing (22:9), or they also fall to the ground but are not said to see or hear anything (26:13–14). It would be superficial simply to remark that Luke neglects historical details and therefore does not mind contradicting himself on such small points. The fact is that Luke does not contradict himself, but makes the same point in three different ways. The point is that there is a radical contrast between Saul and his companions. The discrepancy between their experience and his highlights the state of confusion into which his world and he himself are thrown by the event. The only witnesses cannot witness to anything.

Thus, what began as a journey from life to death, from the life of faithful Judaism to the death of the Christian heretics, ends with Saul's descent into death (symbolized by his blindness), itself preluding to his rising to new life as a follower of Christ who recovers sight through baptism. The myth is thus made of a complex system of permutations in which an original relationship (from + to −) is reversed into its opposite (from − to +).

    Originally (+) marks Jerusalem
                 Saul the leader on horseback
                 Judaism as light
                 Judaism as actively persecuting
                 the journey to Damascus
                 the companions of Saul
    while (−) marks Damascus.
    Finally (−) marks Jerusalem
                 the fallen Saul
                 Judaism as darkness
                 the blinded Saul
                 Saul symbolically dead
                 Saul's unperceiving companions
    while (+) marks Damascus
                 Ananias, who represents both another
                    kind of Judaism and "the Way"
                 Saul recovering sight and life.

    Still to speak in terms of myth, the whole purpose of the story is to explain the miracle through which Saul's inversion of values has taken place. The heart of the myth lies at the crossroads of two movements: from Jerusalem to Damascus as from life to death, and from heavenly light to the grounded blindness of Saul's fall. We may see these as a horizontal and a vertical movement. Their intersection transforms the first, gives it another value, making it into a journey from darkness to light, from Judaism to Christ, or, if we prefer, from the Judaism of the high priest (explicitly mentioned in I—in the singular—and III—in the plural) to that of Ananias.

    But if we focus attention on this transforming moment, we see that in I and II the central event, though already fully decisive, is not quite finalized. Only in III does the full impact of the event appear immediately: here Jesus instructs Saul with a brief but rather full theological treatise on mission and conversion. This is clearly a conflation of what I and II describe as two distinct and complementary moments. Paul does the same thing in Galatians 1:12, where he somewhat contradicts the Lukan account I and II: "It is not a human message that

I was given by men; it is something I learned only through a revelation of Jesus Christ." In I and II, in fact, the appearance of Jesus shatters Saul's world, breaks his self-confidence, forces him into the most basic humiliation of being powerless without help, teaches him to rely on others, and, sending him on to Damascus for further instructions to be received from a man, prepares him to revise all his convictions and to reverse his way of life by following "the way" which he has hitherto persecuted.

In the standard Lukan account, I and II, there are two moments in Saul's conversion. First, Saul meets Jesus in a vision and immediately recognizes him. He sees Jesus as the Son of Man of the apocalyptic tradition. In 1 Corinthians 9:1, Paul argues that his vision made him an apostle, the last one (1 Cor 15:8), yet equal to the others in apostleship, with the same rights as "the other apostles, the Lord's brothers, and Cephas" (1 Cor 9:5). Accounts I and II, however, do not even hint at this. Only III comes near to it, though not quite: if the verb "to send" *(apostello)* is related to the word "apostle," Saul is sent only as "minister and witness" *(hyperete kai martyra)* of what he has seen and of what will be revealed to him.

In I and II, Saul on the way to Damascus learns, through a traumatic experience, the identity of Jesus as the one who now confronts him. Saul the hunter becomes the hunted—hunted by the one he himself hunted in the disciples a moment before—in line with the personal collective identity of the Son of Man in Daniel 7:18. The rest of what Saul learns results from his meeting with Ananias in Damascus. In I, Saul is found by Ananias after an elaborate scenario with a miraculous dream and a vision of the Lord by Ananias. In this version the mission of Saul is revealed to Ananias, not to Saul himself.[9] II places this revelation in the mouth of Ananias speaking to Saul. In both, Saul is instructed and baptized. In I and III, Saul immediately preaches in the synagogues. In II, he returns to Jerusalem, where his mission is confirmed by a vision while he prays in the temple. It is clear that Luke has no knowledge of the sojourn in Arabia mentioned in Galatians 1:17.

If one admits that I and II are roughly correct in dividing Paul's conversion into two phases—on the way and in Damascus—then III, like Galatians 1, telescopes the affair. This is the sort of view that Paul would be likely to adopt when, for personal or apologetic reasons, he argued that his mission came directly from the risen Lord. But if the Lukan account in I and II is correct, then Paul's apostleship does not belong to the original event. It appears after the fact, as a point heatedly but cogently argued by Paul when provoked by the Judaizers who question his preaching to the Gentiles. But one may wonder how soon Paul himself reached the conclusion that he was an apostle—even *the* apostle to the Gentiles—and at what point he discovered the central insight of his preaching, the heart of the Gospel.

In the letters of Paul, 1 Thessalonians certainly antedates the great insight on justification which is fully formulated in Romans. The Thessalonians are exhorted to practice their faith as a kind of new law leading to sanctification (4:2–12). The greater epistles, Galatians, 1 and 2 Corinthians, and Romans, speak another language: Christ himself "has become our wisdom, and our virtue, and our holiness, and our freedom" (1 Cor 1:30). It is "in Christ" rather than through our legal works that we can be justified before God.[10] Thus, Paul's great insight must be dated between 1 Thessalonians and Galatians. 1 Thessalonians, which mentions Macedonia and Achaia, must have been written shortly after Paul carried the Gospel to Achaia and the city of Corinth, while the great Epistles date from Paul's third missionary journey.

Luke's testimony is rather different. Luke, who never clearly explains Paulinism, carefully illustrates its historical context. Paul's preaching in Athens logically followed his previous method, but it was a total failure, which forced him to revise all his conceptions. Important as they were, Paul's experience on the way to Damascus and his subsequent "retreat" with Ananias have not completely restructured his thought. His life henceforth was centered on the risen Christ who, appearing to him as the Son of Man, had become his Lord. Yet Paul remained a Pharisee, though a Christian one, in his teaching. 1 Thessalonians contains samples of his theology before the Athenian experience. In it, Jesus has replaced the Law, but still according to the structures of the Law; the faith is guaranteed by moral conduct; it gives comfort among tribulations; it exists in acts of neighborly love.

Before Athens, Paul approached Jews and proselytes before turning to the Gentiles. He preached "Jesus, that he is the Son of God" (Acts 9:20). To the Jews he spoke of the fulfillment of the prophecies;

to the Gentiles he spoke of salvation. In Athens, according to Luke, Paul preached "Jesus and the resurrection" (17:18). But the story went forth as "Jesus and Anastasis," possibly identified as a god and a goddess: "He seems to be a setter forth of strange gods, for he preaches Jesus and Anastasis" (17:18). Philosophers, Epicureans and Stoics, asked for explanations. Paul then attempted flattering his audience: "I have seen for myself how scrupulous you are in all religious matters . . ." (17:22). He identified Jesus with the "unknown god" to whom an altar on the agora was dedicated. He criticized idolatry, quoted a Greek poet, finally announced a day of repentance, in which the world would be judged by a man designated for that purpose. As told by Luke, the story does not feature the name of Jesus, the mention of his Lordship, or even salvation. It has the form of a friendly appeal to fellow-philosophers, who themselves frequently criticized idol worship. But Greek philosophy balked at the idea of a resurrection of the flesh. And Paul's auditors finally laughed at him: "We would like to hear you talk about this again" (17:32).

In Athens Paul has discovered the utter inadequacy of his apologetics before the wall of Greek culture. And this has shattered the structures of his Christian experience so far. It is of course not his transformation on the way to Damascus which is challenged, but the manner in which Paul has understood its implications and carried them out in his life and preaching.

Only after such an experience can Paul make the unequivocal statement of 1 Corinthians 1:22: "While Jews demand miracles and the Greeks look for wisdom, here are we preaching a crucified Christ; to Jews an unsurmountable obstacle, to pagans madness, but to those who have been called, whether Jews or Greeks, a Christ who is the power and the wisdom of God" (1 Cor 1:22). And again: "As for me, brothers, when I came to you, it was not with any show of oratory or philosophy, but simply to tell you what God had guaranteed. During my stay with you, the only knowledge I claimed to have was about Jesus, and only about him as the crucified Christ" (1 Cor 2:1–2). Only thus can the faith of Paul's listeners rest on "the power of the Spirit" (1 Cor 2:4). Can we not surmise that if Paul insists so much on this aspect of his preaching when he arrived at Corinth, it is partly because this was not the center of his teaching before his fiasco in Athens? And if the Letter to the Galatians speaks so heatedly against the

Judaizers, is it not partly because Paul's preaching in Galatia had unguardedly left open an option for this type of faith? The Gentile "theology of glory" which Paul preached in Athens has its natural counterpart in a theology of glory in the Jewish context, the theology of the Judaizers. But Paul now cares neither for Law nor for philosophy; he will not lower the Gospel to Pharisaic rules or Greek fashions. And while the structures of his new thinking emerge in the Letters to the Galatians and the Corinthians the full display of this restructuring is at the heart of his Letter to the Romans. Here Paul stresses the gratuity of the divine call. Justification results from the gift of "divine grace, coming through the one man, Jesus Christ" (Rom 5:15). The reception of grace is faith. Paul's preaching now leaves aside all human wisdom and announces only the source of grace and the power of faith. Miracles are nothing; philosophy is nothing; but the stark Gospel is that Jesus died on the cross for the salvation of Jews and Gentiles, and rose from the dead. Justification follows neither a Jewish nor a Gentile way; it is by faith, and by faith alone.

I certainly would not maintain that the Athens episode took place just as Luke has reported it. Here again, Luke tries to make a point rather than chronicle the details of events. His point is that somewhere during what we call the second missionary journey, Paul drew the full consequences of his Damascus experience. That Luke places this in Athens may itself be a literary device underlying the contrast between two cities: Athens, the city of Greek culture and lights, and of Paul's confusion, over against Corinth, the city of business and promiscuity, and of Paul's full Gospel. In this case we would have a pattern similar to that between Damascus and Jerusalem.

Originally, (+) marks Athens, the city of wisdom (philosophy) and piety, while (−) marks Corinth, the city with little wisdom (1 Cor 2:26) and despised people (1 Cor 2:28).

Finally, (−) marks Athens, where very few believed (Acts 17:34), the city of Paul's exit (Acts 17:33), while (+) marks Corinth, where many believe (Acts 18:8) and Paul is welcome among both Jews (Acts 18:2) and Gentiles (Acts 18:7).

As in the parallel case of Jerusalem-Damascus, the opposition, Athens-Corinth, illustrates the reversal of values which is entailed by the experience of conversion-justification. Jerusalem-Damascus is limited to conversion; it signifies the passage from Judaism to acknowledgment of Christ. Athens-Corinth deepens the Pauline theology; it signifies the passage from the remnant of a theology of work and glory to the fuller discovery of faith and the cross. The story of Paul's Athenian experience is Luke's way of showing that the insight into justification by faith arose from Paul's sense of fiasco at what ought to have been the crowning point of Paul's proclamation of the Gospel to the Gentiles. If Luke does not fully explain Paul's theology, and may not fully understand it, he is aware of its central point and he provides a context to understand its genesis.[11]

If this reading of Acts is correct, then the doctrine of justification in the great Letters, and especially in the Letter to the Romans, acquires a new dimension. Neither Paul's initial encounter with the risen Christ nor his later conversations with Peter and James sufficed to determine the form of his doctrine. His Pharisaic theology of glory was followed first by another theology of glory, bathed in the perceived glory of Jesus as the apocalyptic Son of Man. Is it not symptomatic that the First Letter to the Thessalonians is basically a letter of congratulations for the faith? The Paul who wrote it had not yet entirely assimilated the idea of dying with Christ; he had not yet experienced anguish as the human ground for receiving divine grace and justice.

On the contrary, Romans, together with Galatians and 1 and 2 Corinthians, teaches the total breakdown of all human religious systems, the catastrophe of the self, before the revelation and communication of divine justice. The model of faith is Abraham, who lived before the Law, and who was justified before he was circumcised. There is faith when life is given to the dead and nothingness is called to existence (4:17), when there is "hope against hope" (4:18). The believers' glorification can only be of Christ and in Christ, who "died for the unjust" (5:6), in whom they are "saved from wrath" (5:9) and through whom they "already have obtained reconciliation" (5:11). God alone "predestines," and "calls," and "justifies," and "glorifies." All this is done through Christ, in the power of the Spirit. And the purpose of God is that "the image of his Son" (8:29) be reproduced in "those who love him" (8:28). But in the dialectic which Paul has now perceived, the image of the Son involves his dying and rising (8:34), so that the moment of dread, the moment of terror and death, is never left behind as a moment of the past that can be remembered but no longer experienced. Only insofar as we are able to perceive in our own nothingness the abysmal fullness of the love of Christ given for us can we "triumph through the one who has loved us" (8:37).

The doctrine of gratuitous justification became, at some time after his Athenian failure, the heart of Paul's Gospel. It is a matter of debate whether Paul's theology was to evolve further, whether the more triumphal tone of Colossians and Ephesians is still his own or belongs to other authors working in the Pauline orbit. I do not see any ultimate objection to their strict Pauline authorship. For as his reflection after his conversion on the way to Damascus took something like twenty years, plus a traumatic experience of failure, to mature, a further development, under the impact of his later apostolate and his several captivities, can hardly be excluded. Yet in this case the enlarged Christological and ecclesial perspectives of the later Letters must be read within Paul's understanding of justification. For there is no evidence that this was left behind. By the nature of things it could not be left behind. Any further development of this theology can only come, as suggested in Philippians 1:11, "when you will reach the perfect goodness which Jesus Christ produces in us for the glory and praise of God."

II.

THE OLDER THEOLOGIES

The full impact of Paul's Athenian experience on his doctrine was lost in the bustling growth of the Church in the first centuries. In fact, commentaries on the Pauline Epistles were not numerous. Origen commented on Romans around 243. John Chrysostom (c. 345–407) preached in Antioch on the Epistle to the Romans with his own moral and pastoral concerns which gave the tone to the oriental theology of grace.[1] In Latin, Marius Victorinus (4th c.), Ambrosiaster (4th c.) and the heretic Pelagius (born c. 400) commented on some or all of Paul's Epistles.[2] But it was with Augustine that the typical Western theology of grace and justification took shape, in reaction, precisely, against Pelagianism.[3] Yet even Augustine did not comment systematically on Paul, even though some of his anti-Pelagian writings deal explicitly with the Epistles to the Galatians and to the Romans. While Paul was highly honored especially as the co-founder with Peter of the Church in Rome, there is no evidence that he was given special importance in the theology of justification during the great patristic period.

Patristic teaching in general stressed two apparently antinomic points made in the Gospel of John. On the one hand, "No one can come to me unless the Father, who has sent me, draw him" (Jn 6:44). On the other, "the one who loves me shall be loved by my Father" (Jn 14:21) and also, "The one who does the truth comes to the light" (Jn 3:21). "Doing the truth" served to suggest the possibility of even pagan religion, in its higher forms, acting as a stepping-stone to faith. The case of the centurion Cornelius could be taken as a paradigm of the way in which God rewards the virtuous life of pagans. Grace is of course necessary for salvation, but one gets the impression that divine grace may be attracted by good works previously made in the light of one's unaided conscience. Such an approach was related to the experience of conversion which of course was widespread before the Constantinian transformation of the Church.[4] It generally prevailed in both East and West before Augustine. From reading Tertullian, Hilary, and Ambrose, as well as Gregory of Nyssa or John Chrysostom, one could conclude that, while justification results only from divine grace, yet it is possible for human persons to prepare its reception. There was no systematic attempt, however, to analyze the possible steps of such a preparation.

An illustration of this pre-Augustinian theology may be provided by Hilary of Poitiers' account of his own conversion. A bishop of Poitiers in Gaul, Hilary (315–367), who came to the faith as an adult, describes his conversion at the beginning of his work, *On the Trinity.* He was led, he testifies, by a desire for the good and a search for the truth. As for many others in the culture of his times, who were vaguely influenced by various forms of Platonism, the good meant for him the right way of life leading to blessed immortality. Hilary could not believe that death was the last word about human life: "Life was not given by God just in view of death, for it did not seem proper to a Good Giver to grant the joyful feeling of life for the sake of *(ad)* the sad fear of death."[5] While in this state of mind, Hilary, reading the Old Testament, was impressed by its doctrine of God, especially regarding the divine attributes: "I plainly admired such an absolute teaching about God."[6] Later, he found in the Gospel according to John a conception of the Word which no pagan philosophy had even suspected:

> My mind reached beyond the understanding available to the natural intellect, and was taught about God more than it knew before. It learnt from God that God was its Creator; it heard that the Word was God and with God at the beginning. It came to know the light of the world present in the world and unrecognized by the world.[7]

This discovery of the biblical doctrine of God brought Hilary to a hope unknown in paganism. "Here my tense and anxious mind found more than it expected." For if God is our Creator, our Father, then our divine filiation is not a fatality imposed upon us; it is a vocation opened to us by the incarnation of the Word of God. "The Word was made flesh so that through the Word made flesh the flesh might make progress toward the divine Word." Thus Hilary was freed from the fear of eternal extinction in death. Such a deep experience of newness and liberation was in fact considered by the Church Fathers to be the normal outcome of the Christian message. It provided the basis for apologetic. We are no longer under the blind dominion of fate, but we have come under the fatherhood of the Creator, who has given us salvation in his Son, the eternal Word who was made flesh so that all flesh might reach God.

The proper response to this good news is faith. Hilary calls it "the most absolute faith of this confession of piety," the "solid faith which rejects captious and useless philosophical questions."[8] Such a faith implies obedience, as Hilary expresses it in a very dense formulation: "The task of religion is the office of obedience."[9] Even for an intellectual like Hilary, who was attracted to Christianity because he was searching for philosophical truth, faith is no mere intellectual assent; it is more than knowledge; it is hope. Conversion requires harmony between our life and this hope, a harmony which is to be found in the Christian community through obedience. This entails conformity of behavior with the truth, acceptance of the Church's authority, the fulfillment of one's calling. For Hilary this in fact meant, as he himself says, being ordained to the priesthood "by the ministry of the designated bishop."

Placing Hilary's autobiographical reflections in the context of the theology of grace, we see that his accession to faith, prepared by his philosophical quest, inspired the good works of his Christian life. Hence the general principle, formulated in his *Commentary on the Psalms:* "To remain in the faith is indeed God's gift, but to begin has its origin in ourselves." And also: "It belongs to the divine mercy to help those who have the will, to strengthen beginners, to receive those who come; but from us is the beginning, so that God may perfect it."[10] This translates Hilary's experience as he saw it. The medieval axiom, *Facienti quod in se est Deus non denegat gratiam* (To those who do what is in them God does not deny grace), is already here in substance. Divine grace is from God and is necessary to salvation, but persons of good will can prepare for it.

Practically all the Church Fathers before Augustine took a similar position on the human capacity to prepare for the gift of grace.[11] As they wrote largely with the necessity for radical *metanoia,* conversion, in mind, this should cause no surprise. The concern for orthodoxy of faith, so patent in the Councils, stressed the noetic aspect of belief,[12] yet it never ruled out in early, pre-Pelagian practices, a proper cooperation of the human will. This was in line with the better philosophies of the time, which presented themselves as systems of behavior leading to a morally and culturally good life. As Gustave Bardy showed in his study of conversion in the early Church, the passage from paganism to Christianity did not always, perhaps not often, give the impression of total transformation.[13] The *metanoia* of the Christian worked itself out progressively. Baptismal grace indeed gave new life, but not without previous preparation. We have seen it in Hilary's case. With Augustine, and in spite of what is said in the *Confessions* about his evil ways before his conversion, there was a process of growth. It is even difficult to determine the exact moment of his conversion. Before being baptized in 387, Augustine underwent philosophical conversions, first to Manichaeanism, then to neo-Platonism.[14] If his experience of being justified by grace coincided approximately with his asking for and receiving baptism, it is clear that he had been on the way for some time. Thus the patristic theology of justification is inseparable from the experience of conversion as a process in which the human search for wisdom and the good life plays a positive role. Augustine himself followed this line of thought in his early Christian writings, before he became a bishop (396). Later, the teachings of Pelagius struck him as constituting a major heresy which threatened the reality of grace and thereby the sovereignty of the Word of God. He duly corrected his earlier approach in his *Retractions* (426–427).[15]

Pelagius, a monk from the British Isles, had come to prominence in Rome as a distinguished spiritual guide. He even was a commentator on the Epistles of Paul, and he stressed the importance of "faith alone" for the justification of the sinner. But his problem was no longer that of conversion to Christianity. His clientele in the Christian layers of the Roman population was found among those who aspired to the ascetic life, the life of holiness as it came to popularity after the age of the martyrs, when the hero or model of Christian life was the hermit, the ascetic, the virgin. The main problem is not justification; it is sanctification, how to live in the world as not of the world. Pelagius could then distinguish more clearly than was customary before him between the grace of faith and baptism, which effects justification, and the post-baptismal grace of doing good works in keeping with the virtuous life. Besides and after the grace of faith, there must be room for "the works of faith." If justice is given basically with baptism, each person must fulfill in life the "works of justice." Thus, Pelagius does not deny the power of grace. He admits to its necessity for the initiation, for the conversion of baptism. But he denies it for the works of the believer. He establishes a double system of justification. Initial justice is due solely to grace through faith; continuing justice derives from ascetical efforts and achievements. There is no human self-sufficiency for salvation; yet there is a Christian self-sufficiency for holiness.[16]

Augustine's first version of his developed theory of grace was formulated in his *Letter to Simplicianus*, Ambrose's successor in Milan, in 397. Augustine actually began this letter with the intention of defending free will against its detractors, as he confesses in the *De praedestinatione sanctorum* (429). But he found himself discovering that true liberty can only be utterly dependent on divine grace. That this was indeed a discovery is patent from Augustine's language: "The grace of God won." Augustine was persuaded by "the apostolic testimony," that is, by reflection on 1 Corinthians 4:7: "What do you have that you have not received? And if you have received it, why do you boast as though it were your own?" He even says that the solution of the problem of free will was, on that occasion, "revealed" to him by God.[17] Revelation, here, is not to be taken in its formal sense. There was no private revelation to Augustine, but there was an insight into the meaning of the Gospel as explained by Paul. All good is from God. Accordingly, there can be no self-preparation for grace. At all moments of the Christian life and of its search for holiness, there is the gift and the power of divine grace. The same solution must apply to the situation of the Christian being sanctified and that of the pagan being brought to faith: both events result totally from grace.

The more involved he became in his polemic against the followers of Pelagius, the more clearly did Augustine perceive the consequences of the principle of grace. All humanity suffers under sin. Original sin is not only that of Adam. Certainly, Augustine taught that through Adam all human nature had been corrupted, all flesh had become disobedient. All men, being born from the disobedience of the flesh, can only belong to the devil, "because they are born through the desire in which the flesh desires against the spirit and obliges the spirit to desire against it."[18] This contamination reaches all descendants of Adam, whatever their age. Admittedly, this is not easy to understand. Nothing, he remarks, "is more important to preach, nothing harder to understand."[19] To Julian of Eclana, the arch-Pelagian, he enjoins: "If you can, understand; if you cannot, believe."[20] At any rate it follows that the actions performed under the impact of sin are themselves sinful. As these acquire their own influence, each person inherits a host of original sins. This cumulative effect is such that only God's intervention, his free grace, can break the fatal cycle. Not only is it impossible to achieve or merit one's own salvation, but the human will, left to its resources, would effectively tend to evil. On reflection Augustine could appeal to his experience, as recorded in the *Confessions*. By implication he could also appeal, along with Paul, to universal human experience. Even before the Pelagian crisis he could write: "All who are born in mortality endure the wrath of God."[21] Whether this should be called pessimism or realism largely depends on the prevailing cultural trends. Augustine, who witnessed the beginning of the break-up of the Roman Empire, viewed it as realistic.

The doctrine of original sin and its transmission gives a framework for the dark side of Augustinianism. Humanity, unredeemed, is a *massa damnata*. Only the elect, predestined to salvation, escape it eventually; the others are predestined to damnation by a just judgment of God which we cannot fathom. But there is a bright side. If, in its post-lapsarian state—and historical humanity knows no other—the human will has become radically sinful, God alone is the source of all good. The field of the divine goodness includes creation and humanity. If divine grace is absolutely necessary for salvation, it is also effectively given to those whom God has chosen. It comes as a totally undeserved, unprepared gift from God. The radicality of the gift extends, as it were, both backward and forward. Backward, one must recognize that even the very first movement of conversion is due to grace; this point is clearly made in *De correptione et gratia* (426). Forward, one can see that grace bears good fruits in the Christian life. It is an action of God, an interior appeal of the Word, a solicitation of the Holy Spirit. It does not call the faithful to passivity, but it awakens them to the true good and leads them to the truly blessed life. It is therefore responsible for the works of a good life. "Men are acted upon in order to act, not in order to do nothing."[22] Augustine himself, in his sermons, urged thé people to good works. He also favored asceticism, requiring celibacy from his clergy and even a community life in a presbyterium organized like a monastery, encouraging the virgins in their chosen style of living. But the basis he saw for this was not in an assumed capacity of the post-baptismal efforts to control the wayward tendencies of the heart. It was in the ties between grace and love. *Caritas* was the love born of faith. The movement which makes man *ex malo bonum* (from evil, good) is not from man; it is "from him and through him and in him who always is good."[23] And it does not end before "the tree bears good fruits." This is Paul's "faith working out in love" (Gal 5:6). Augustine sees the works of love as being themselves the works of faith, whose efficacy is due solely to the grace without which there can be neither love nor faith.

Thanks to Augustine's efforts, Pelagianism was condemned at the Council of Carthage in 418. The Council affirmed both the universal extension of original sin (canons 1–2) and the universal necessity of grace (canons 4–8).[24] Yet it is unfortunate that the position of the Council was couched in the negative terms of condemnations rather than in a positive explanation of doctrine. The teaching of Augustine was richer than what was said explicitly at the Council of Carthage. Augustine taught a new theology. But he did so through his recovery of the Pauline insight in its radical thoroughness. What Augustine came to affirm had already been said by Paul. But returning to a half-forgotten older theology was a challenge to the contemporary ascetical trends.

As events showed, the theology of Augustine was in fact too radical for some of those who, engaged in the ascetical life and schooled in the old ways, had not perceived the dangers of Pelagianism. There were monks in southern Gaul who considered Augustine excessively pessimistic about the natural desire for God. This monastic reaction may be illustrated with a quotation from Faustus of Riez (c. 408–c. 490): "This alone is ours, that, being incapacitated by our frailty, at best we may placate [God] through the importunity of our searching and knocking."[25] One can prepare for divine grace, at least to the extent of desiring it. Thus the question was raised again of the first moment of conversion, of the first movement toward faith. If the human search for God can reach God insofar as God makes himself available to those who seek him, the beginning of salvation lies in the human heart itself. Such an interpretation of religious experience, usually called semi-Pelagianism, counters the Augustinian conception of grace. If salvation is necessarily the work of grace alone, must not the very first movement toward salvation be also attributed to grace?

The affirmative answer was given by the Second Council of Orange (529). Largely under the influence of Caesarius of Arles (c. 469–542) and Prosper of Aquitaine (first half of 5th c.) this local Council adopted a position which may be called strict Augustinianism. According to its canon 5, even the first movement of faith results from the Holy Spirit. There is an "inspiration . . . which makes our will pass from infidelity to faith and from impiety to piety."[26] Canon 6 speaks of an "infusion and inspiration of the Holy Spirit," canon 7 of an "illumination and inspiration of the Holy Spirit." Canon 6 lists a number of acts which cannot be performed without this inspiration: "When we believe, we want, we desire, we try, we toil, we pray, we watch, we study, we ask, we seek, we knock." Were this enumeration reversed, it could provide a fairly exhaustive description of the psychological process of coming to faith. But this is not the purpose of the canon. The purpose is to assert that the least of these acts, in which faith is somehow anticipated, is itself the product of divine grace. It is not, as the canon goes on, humility or obedience which attracts divine grace; but grace makes us obedient and humble. The Council does not deny that some naturally good actions may not result from grace. Yet these are not made *sicut oportet* (canon 5 and 6), as required for salvation. It is not "without the illumination and inspiration of the Holy Spirit" that one can "conceive, *ut expedit* (as is necessary), what pertains to the salvation of eternal life, or choose it, or assent to the salvific, evangelical, proclamation. . . ." In fact, it is only the Holy Spirit "who gives to all the unction of consenting to and believing the truth" (canon 7). The ascent to faith is alone of its kind; it exists only *sicut oportet, ut expedit,* in keeping with the nature of evangelical truth, with the Gospel.

Orange II was not a general Council. Yet its doctrine was endorsed, in 531, by Pope Boniface II (530–532). Writing to Caesarius of Arles, who had sent him the acts of the Council with the request that he would "confirm" the true faith "with the authority of the apostolic see," the bishop of Rome stated:

> It is certain and catholic that in regard to all good things *(in omnibus bonis),* the chief *(caput)* of which is faith, divine mercy precedes us when still unwilling, so that we may will; it is present in us as we will; it also follows so that we may remain in faith. . . .[27]

Thus, divine grace or mercy enfolds every goodness on the believer's part; there is no good, for the Christian, without grace. We should of course not be misled by the translation, "good things." The question is not just one of performing good actions. *Bona* designates all good, whether in the action or in the being of a Christian. All such good is due to divine grace, including the first good, which is faith. The vocabulary is more popular than technical. Yet the intent is clear. It does not classify faith among the things to be willed; this would make it a human work, even though inspired by grace. Rather, the voluntaristic vocabulary evokes the fullness of personal conversion, along the lines of Augustine's conception of the good act, which involves the whole person turning to God, but this turning is the effect of divine grace, not of the human person. The Roman text implicitly subsumes salvation and sanctification among the *bona* which are embedded in prevenient, accompanying and following grace, but also the very act of being made just before God, which we call justification.

The canons of Orange constitute a major step in the transmission of the Pauline tradition. Yet it is puzzling how little these canons were known to subsequent centuries. The theologians of the ninth century were still acquainted with them. In fact, Hincmar of Reims (845–882) quoted them twenty times in his polemics against Gottschalk concerning predestination.[28] One finds what could be allusions to the semi-Pelagian controversy in the thirteenth century: the Franciscan Matthew of Aquasparta (c. 1237–1302) mentions what he calls the "neo-Pelagians."[29] But neither he nor any of the Scholastic authors quotes the canons of Orange. Thomas Aquinas apparently obtained a knowledge of this Council between 1259 and 1269.[30] The first theologian actually to quote the canons directly is the Spaniard Andrew de Vega, in 1546.[31] This is of course a very late date, posterior in fact to the position of the problem of justification by the first reformers. The reason for this ignorance is that none of the great collections of Canon Law included the canons of Orange. These are neither in Gratianus' *Decretum* (1150) nor in the older collections, such as the *Dionysio-Hadriana* or the *Hispana*. Hincmar, who had made extensive researches in the manuscripts of the theologians and canonists during the controversy over predestination, knew them from a small collection containing mainly conciliar texts from southern Gaul.[32] But for whatever reasons, the canons of Orange did not pass into later canonical collections, until they finally came to be included in that of Peter of Crabbe, published in Cologne in 1538.[33] This was too late to prevent the problems of the Reformation. There was an information gap concerning the Council of Orange from the tenth to the sixteenth century.

But does this imply that the doctrine of Orange was itself in eclipse during this long period? The situation is in fact not clear. Indeed, early medieval commentaries on the Epistles of Paul generally identify the "justice of God" of Romans 1:17 as God's justice made present in us and acting out our justification as God's entire doing. But it is one thing to read a statement out of Scripture; it is another to make this statement an active principle in theology. In fact, the predestinarian controversy of the ninth century shows a distinct divergence between the writers and bishops of southern Gaul (chiefly those of the ecclesiastical province of Lyon)[34] and those of the north (led by Hincmar, archbishop of Reims), in their interpretation of the position of St. Augustine against the Pelagians.

Gottschalk (c. 803–869), a Saxon monk of Orbais, and thus himself a northerner, took a strict view of Augustinian orthodoxy: God has predestined all men; Christ did not die for the damned but only for the elect; there is no free will in the sinner; justification is entirely God's action, without any active human cooperation. He used and supported the formula of Isidore of Sevilla (c. 570–636) that there is a *gemina predestinatio*.[35] Divine predestination, as Gottschalk explained it, is one in God, at its origin, and twofold in its effects, among men: some are predestined to eternal glory, others to eternal death.

Concerned about the pastoral consequences of such a teaching, Hincmar intervened. The archbishop of Mainz, Raban Maur (776–856), who had condemned the doctrines of Gottschalk in 849, sent

Gottschalk, expelled from King Louis' lands, to the province of Reims, where he had been ordained.[36] In 849 therefore, Hincmar, following the canons, called a provincial synod to examine Gottschalk's teaching. This was done at a Synod of Quiersy (849) whose acts have now been lost. Gottschalk was condemned and confined to a monastery at Hautvillers. The predestinarian controversy as such started when other theologians, including some bishops, supported Gottschalk. At another Synod of Quiersy (853), called, it seems, by King Charles the Bald, four articles of doctrine were adopted.[37] The first affirms that man sinned freely, and that, out of the ensuing mass of perdition, God "elected those he predestined to life"; there is only one predestination, because, if a just damnation is predestined to the others, these are not predestined to their evil choice. The second affirms that free will, lost in the first man, has been recovered through Christ: "and when it is oriented to and supported by grace, we use free will for the good; when it is abandoned by grace, for evil. We have free will because it has been freed by grace and restored to health by grace, from corrupted that it was." The third affirms the universal salvific will of God, although not all are in fact saved. The fourth affirms that Christ died for all men, although in fact not all men are saved by his death. These last two articles attribute to human free will the failure to be saved.

Clearly enough, the second article is highly questionable from an Augustinian point of view. For it attributes to their own free will the good performed by the elect. A carefully anti-Pelagian doctrine would attribute it to divine grace. Hence the violent reaction of the ecclesiastical province of Lyon, a reaction which surprised Hincmar immensely. Hincmar indeed thought he was faithful to the tradition. In fact, along with others among the theologians involved, he used pseudo-Augustinian material, among which the *Hypomnesticon.* He even used the *De induratione cordis pharaoni,* which he believed to be by St. Jerome, but which actually was a work of Pelagius himself.[38] Thus Hincmar thought that he stood in the great patristic tradition when he defended not only the oneness of predestination, but also the personal capacity to do what is good after the will, previously caught in the *massa damnata,* has been healed by baptismal grace.

There is no need for us to follow all the intricacies of the controversy, the exchange of polemical writings, Hincmar's strenuous search for manuscripts, and the nuanced position of John Scot Eriugena (c.

810–877), the greatest theologian of the time, who opposed both Gottschalk and Hincmar.[39] While rejecting the non-universality of the mystery of the cross, the southerners argued against Hincmar, on the basis of their better knowledge of Augustine. Their position was well summed up at the Council of Valence (855). Here it is accepted that there is "a predestination to life of the elect, and a predestination to death of the impious," in such a way, however, that "the mercy of God precedes the merited good," whereas "the merited evil precedes the just judgment of God" (canon 3). Furthermore, "concerning grace, through which the faithful are saved and without which a rational creature never lives in blessedness, and concerning free will, diseased through sin in the first man," the Council abides by the decisions of "the synods of Africa and Orange." The Synod of Africa was the anti-Pelagian Council of Carthage of 418. The four articles of Quiersy were blamed for their "ineptitude," and their arguments were called "the devil's commentary," expressions which were obviously not calculated to placate Hincmar.[40]

After more writings on all sides, the end of the controversy came with the agreement of the Synod of Douzy (860). While Quiersy had been a northern Synod and the membership of Valence is unknown, but presumably southern, Douzy was representative of fourteen provinces; it was, so to say, an all-Gallic Council. But was a solution truly arrived at? Although the profession of faith of Douzy does not employ Quiersy's language about the post-baptismal freedom of the will, it goes much further than either Valence or Orange in asserting the free will of the baptized and its capacity to do good. After a long description of God's omnipotence, the text goes on to say that God "wants no one to perish," that "after the fall of the first man God does not want to take away violently the free choice of his will *(suae voluntatis liberum arbitrium)*," that to all men God "is prepared to give what is just."[41] It also states that, according to the Scriptures,

> because, after the fall of the first man, there is in man, in order to will the good, to begin it and bring it to completion, and to persevere in it, a will *(liberum arbitrium),* freed by grace, healed by grace from corruption, by grace preceded, assisted, and destined to be crowned, man, deficient in the good and tending to evil, has, after the fall of the first man, a free will, that is, free from justice

and servant of sin. . . . Hence, because there is the grace of God, the world is saved; and because there is free will in man, the world will be judged.[42]

Further below, Christ is called "the head, light, and example of all the predestined." Redemption is said to be "for those who were under the law of sin and of future death." Because of sin "there was made of all humankind a mass of perdition."[43] The text finally elaborates at length on the power of the grace of God, which was at work "from Abel the just," preparing the advent of "the light of the world," and on the redemptive incarnation, described in strongly Trinitarian language.

This is clearly a compromise. The northerners had defended the possibility for Christians of doing good, and for all men that of passing from the damned to the elect and vice versa, though in this case not without divine grace. They wanted to maintain that God is just in both electing and condemning. Their theology was not unlike that of the Fathers before Pelagius. The southerners opposed all that resembled Pelagianism, wanted above all to avoid teaching the self-sufficiency of man for salvation, and explicitly professed fidelity to Augustine's theology of grace. The rather involved language of Douzy gives victory to neither side. It strongly insists on grace and on the Christological aspect of salvation. But it stresses equally that it is the will—freed by grace—which wills, begins, brings to completion, perseveres in, the good. The nature of justification, as the moment when one passes from sin to grace, seems to be clearly perceived as God's entire work through Christ in the Holy Spirit. But the effect of justification is not clearly analyzed. The possibility of divergent views on the power of the redeemed for sanctification remains. One suspects that agreement was reached, not because either side persuaded the other, but because of general exhaustion. Perhaps a lesson can be learned from this remote controversy. Both sides intended to express the orthodox doctrine. But orthodoxy may be approached from two different angles. One may look at the problems of justice, justification, and good works ontologically; in themselves, they can only be from God, sinful man being unable to do good of himself, even under grace, after baptism and faith. Justification, then, is perceived as an *ontic* event known only through faith. One may also look at such problems psychologically:

the works that one does, the faith that one professes, have to be one's own, if one is truly justified by grace. Then, justification is seen as a process within the believer's life. The predestinarian controversy resulted from a clash of these two tendencies. Whether one should have primacy remains a moot point, which the controversy did nothing to settle.

There is thus sufficient evidence for the conclusion that, due to the unsettled character of the predestinarian controversy, the Carolingians legated to the Middle Ages a confused situation in regard to the understanding of justification and, consequently, to the conception and practice of Christian holiness. The lines between God's grace and human action, God's gift and human responsibility, God's dominion and human will were left unclear. This unclarity could accommodate several theologies of grace, going from Augustine's, if not Gottschalk's, predestinarianism to conceptions that were leaning to, though not identical with, semi-Pelagianism.

At the dawn of the Scholastic period, a new handicap was introduced into the problem of justification by shifts of the semantic field. The civilization of the Middle Ages was giving unique importance to *justitia* as the social bond *par excellence*. By the end of the eleventh century, the feudal organization which had been taking shape since the ninth century was well established. The division between masters and slaves, inherited from antiquity, had vanished, yet social relationships were still cast in terms of dominion and loyalty or obedience. A system of real dominion, based on the ownership of men, services, and lands, had been replaced by a system of juridical dominion. The social link was now guaranteed less by power than by justice as determined by law or, in the absence of law, by custom. Thus justice acquired extraordinary importance as the social virtue *par excellence*. It was presumably not by accident that justice was also prominent in the Church's penitential system. While Communion had become relatively rare, medieval piety practiced the sacrament of penance abundantly. The penitentials—manuals for confessors—transmitted a monastic tradition which derived from the Irish monks. They encouraged a presumption that some proportional balance could and should be established between sins committed and the absolution received, and that the best way to do it was through works of satisfaction. One

may argue whether this was to satisfy the Church of the sinner's penitential contrition, or to satisfy divine justice. In any case, justice, here
again, regulated the religious life of the people.

In these conditions, it was to be expected that, sooner or later, the
heart of the Christian covenant would be expressed in terms of *justitia*. No one did it more effectively than Anselm of Canterbury (1033/
34–1109) in his study of redemption, *Cur Deus homo*. The first part
of this book establishes the philosophical-theological basis for Christian belief in the redemptive incarnation of the Word of God. Intend-
ing to persuade Jews and Moslems, Anselm avoids references to revelation. He formulates his argument within the framework of what he
takes to be necessary reason, persuasive to all rational persons. We are
now equally far from the patristic background in the experience of
metanoia and from the ninth century's wavering between predestination and free will.

The voluntarism of Anselm is unhesitant. What is *justitia?* *Justitia,* also called "the uprightness of the will, which makes the just,
those who are right in their heart, that is, in their will," consists in
"the will of the rational creature being subject to God's will."[44] Justice
is thus closely related to will, both in God and in the rational creatures.
God's will has imposed a law on humankind, and to this law all human
wills must conform. But all have sinned. Humankind has become what
Anselm prefers to call, rather than Augustine's *massa damnata,* a
massa peccatrix.[45] Each one's punishment will be measured by each
one's departure from the law. Anselm, who is fond of quantitative
terms, explains how punishment is measured: "No one ignores that
men's *justitia* stands under a law, so that the measure of punishment
is counted according to its quantity."[46] In other words, the measure of
punishment is in the human will's disobedience to the law. Much of
Cur Deus homo consists in showing that this quantity is infinite and
that, consequently, neither man nor angel can atone properly to satisfy
the demands of justice.

Reversing the perspective, Anselm is therefore led to assert that
the *justitia* which is acceptable to God can only come from God. "No
man has the truth which he teaches, or a just will, from self but from
God."[47] There is an extrinsic or forensic quality about justice: it is not
from man; it is from God. The Christian indeed has a positive relationship to true justice, in faith, and this faith includes both love and

hope. In the dialogue-form of *Cur Deus homo,* Anselm's pupil, Boso, has acknowledged that he has nothing to offer God for his own salvation, except his efforts to lead a holy life in his monastery. He has confessed his powerlessness to save himself: "If I owe myself and my capacity to God even when I am not sinning, I have nothing left to offer for my sin." Anselm then asks: "What then will happen to you? How can you be saved?" Boso, in his answer, contrasts natural reason and faith:

> Considering the reasons you have given me, I do not see how. But turning to my faith, I hope that I can be saved in the Christian faith, "which works through love" (Gal 5:6), and, since we read: "if the unjust be converted from injustices and do justice," that all injustices can fall into oblivion.[48]

The second part of *Cur Deus homo* explains how this is effected through Jesus Christ. Anselm is very much aware of the extrinsic nature of the new *justitia* obtained from God through the Redeemer. Can it be called our own? Only in a remote and limited sense. Anselm, at this point, refers to an angel, but he invokes a universal principle. The angel "could have removed *justitia* from himself, and did not." Only in this indirect sense does he "have *justitia* from himself, for a creature cannot have *justitia* from self in any other way."[49] Likewise, unredeemed man, who is a sinner, can obtain no justice from self. In the redeemed Christian, justice is from self only insofar as this Christian has not removed it by sin. Justice does not really belong to him; it is from God.

I have spoken of a handicap in Anselm's doctrine. Measuring divine justice quantitatively opens the way to legalistic assessments of both justice and injustice. Instead of grace being God's infinitely loving action in sinful humanity, grace is measured. Anselm has happily underlined the gratuitousness of God's gift; he has ruined every human attempt at self-redemption. But by evaluating redemption in terms of legal satisfaction, he has strengthened a juridical tendency which was already latent in Latin theology. He has of course not suspected that the laws of *justitia,* which he applies to the divine attribute of justice no less than to the exercise of justice in human society, are themselves the product of society. He has unwittingly imposed a human pattern on God's action. But if grace is, as it were, a by-product of justice, then justification becomes a mathematical operation proportional to the dimension of sin, a fact which became all too obvious in the later practice of indulgences.[50]

Anselm's doctrine on justification, however, is clarified in two writings, the *De libero arbitrio*, probably composed between 1080 and 1085, and his last work, *De concordia praescientiae et praedestinationis, et gratiae cum libero arbitrio*, of 1107–1108. In both tractates Anselm argues from a conception of freedom as the power to act *(Omnis libertas est potestas)* and of will (called indifferently *arbitrium* and *voluntas*) as the power of self-determination.[51] His interest in dialectics alerts him to the ambiguities of language. He is aware that the word *voluntas* is equivocal: it can denote the instrument of willing—what a faculty psychology will call the faculty of the will—and also the act of willing. As instrument, the will is always present in the soul, and always sovereign. It stands above temptation even when it falls, for it always remains a power of total self-determination. "Everyone who wills wills his own willing."[52] When it comes to freedom of the will, Anselm follows the thought of Augustine. He defines free will not as the power to choose whatever it wants to choose, but as the power to choose the right decision for the sake of righteousness itself. Free will seeks *rectitudinem voluntatis propter ipsam rectitudinem* (righteousness of the will for its own sake).[53] It is not indifferent to good and evil; it is not a-moral. It is radically moral and good. Yet it exists in "angels and men" only because it has been "made by, and accepted from, God."[54] The conditions of its use in sinful humanity, however, are not fully investigated; and so one may be given a superficial impression of Pelagianism.

Such an impression, however, is entirely dispelled by the second of these tractates. The question of the will is now envisaged in the context of justice. What is justice? It is "the righteousness of the will for its own sake."[55] As such, it is not "natural," that is, it does not follow any law of necessity due to nature. It exists only where it is chosen "by the will itself." Anselm's voluntarism is still strongly emphasized: the will is self-determining. The equivocity of the word is still recognized. It is even amplified, for Anselm speaks now of a third denotation of the term. There is "the instrument of willing." There is also "the inclination of the instrument" *(affectus instrumenti)*, which is twofold, since the will can desire both what is useful and what is right. There is, finally, "the use of the instrument," which is as manifold as the actions to choose from.[56] Yet these diverse denotations of the word connote the same basic reality, self-determination.

The problem of grace and free will comes from Scripture itself. Anselm posits it clearly:

> The question arises because holy Scripture sometimes speaks so that free choice *(liberum arbitrium)* seems not to be useful for salvation, but grace alone; sometimes so that all our salvation resides in our free will *(in libera nostra voluntate)*.

Perplexed by such contradictory readings of Scripture, "there are many in our time who despair that *liberum arbitrium* be anything."[57] Anselm's solution does not lie in scriptural exegesis, but in a dialectical analysis of the act of willing what is right.

In this analysis, Anselm finds that choosing the right for its own sake is not what makes the will just. Rather, the opposite is true: the will makes this choice because it is already just. "The will is not right because it wills rightly, but it wills rightly because it is right." "I say that it cannot will rectitude, unless it has the rectitude by which to will it." And again: "In willing, no one is able to obtain it (rectitude) by oneself, because one cannot want it unless one has it." Where does this justice come from? Since it originates neither in oneself nor in "another creature," "it follows that no creature has the rectitude which I have called rectitude of the will, except by grace."[58]

On the strength of the divine origin of the justice of the will, Anselm anticipates in some measure the imputation language which will be dear to the reformers in the sixteenth century. Taking his cue from Romans 9:16 ("So it is not a question of man's willing or running, but of God's mercy") he comments: " . . . it is not denied that in the one who wills and the one who runs free will *(liberum arbitrium)* contributes something, but the meaning is that it is not to free will that one should impute the willing and the running, but to grace."[59] Anselm is aware that many factors may lead sinners to conversion. Yet in this process, as he points out, all is grace:

> Preaching is grace, for what derives from grace is grace; and hearing is grace; and understanding what has been heard is grace; and rectitude of willing is grace.[60]

Through baptismal grace "original injustice" is dismissed; "the guilt of impotence and total corruption . . . is ignored. After baptism they will be blamed for none of the guilt which was in them before baptism, although the corruption itself and the desire which are the punishment of sin are not immediately erased in baptism; and no sin *(delictum)* will be imputed to them after baptism, except what they will have done of their own will."[61]

Admittedly, Anselm speaks of sin not being imputed to the sinner, and of righteousness not being imputed to him, but to grace. To impute means, in his case, to trace the origin back to. It says nothing about whether the soul is intrinsically transformed under grace. It is also compatible with a certain notion of merit. Anselm even uses the two words in one breath:

> That through the merit of faith and hope we might more gloriously obtain the blessedness which we desire, we remain, as long as we are in this life, in that which is no longer imputed as sin, although it did proceed from sin.[62]

More specifically, merit is connected with the second meaning of the word, "will." It has to do with inclinations or affections, with that which the will chooses when it seeks for the useful and for the right: "From these two inclinations, which we also call wills, all human merit proceeds, both good and evil."[63]

A theology inspired by Anselm could not condone any form of semi-Pelagianism. Reversely, opposition to his understanding of redemption could well inflate the human claim to self-sufficiency. It is presumably not by accident that Peter Abelard (1079–1142) both proposed another soteriology, and abandoned the strict position of Augustine in regard to sin and grace. Rather than atonement, redemption was the setting of a unique example, proposed to imitation in the life of faith. Abelard mitigated the gravity of original sin, transmitted as punishment, but not as guilt.[64] He held that sinners can actively prepare themselves for grace. Under the guidance of St. Bernard (c. 1090–1153), a strict Augustinian in the matter of grace, the Council of Sens (1140 or 1141) condemned several propositions attributed to Abelard, notably that "free will *(liberum arbitrium)* suffices of itself to the good."[65] These speculations of Abelard were tied to the Christological discussions of the twelfth century rather than to a debate about grace. Yet they effectively posited the problem of grace as it was to be faced by the great Scholastics.

This is of course not to say that St. Paul was no longer understood. To give one instance, Peter Lombard (d. c. 1160) duly noted the total gratuity of redemption and justification in his *Ordinariae glossae,* which are a brief commentary on Scripture.[66] The Lombard, however, who was influenced by Abelard in his Christology, read Paul in the light of an Augustinian theology of grace, as one can gather from his *Sentences.* This of course raises the question whether justification ought to be looked at in the light of the theology of grace, or divine grace in the light of the experience of justification.

The first Scholastic generation inherited both the Augustinian tradition, recently upheld by Bernard and the Council of Sens, and nagging questions concerning the preparation for grace, whether in the sinner being brought to justification, or in the Christian in the process of sanctification. In fact, the early Scholastics were divided in their answers. Strict Augustinianism was maintained in the school of St. Victor and by Gilbert Porretanus (c. 1080–1154) and his disciples. But, by and large, the opinion of Stephen Langton (c. 1150–1228) was shared by the majority of authors: good actions performed even outside of charity are effective *ad gratiae habilitatem,* "to give a capacity for grace." Stephen was consistent with himself, since he also asserted what had been denied by Orange: all men "have from themselves what is necessary to arise" from sin.[67] While not all would share this humanistic generosity, the feeling that the sinner must at least turn away from sin on his own in order to receive God's grace was frequently expressed, though some saw the result as a negative preparation, like removing an obstacle, others, more positively, as positing a stepping stone for grace. This sort of final pre-grace activity, whether seen as negative or as positive, was embodied in the famous formula current at the beginning of the thirteenth century: *Facienti quod in se est Deus non denegat gratiam* (To the one who does what is in him God does not deny grace). The early Scholastics made various attempts to square together the gratuity of justification, the possibility, even the necessity, of some preparation for grace, and the capacity to merit grace, at least in the sense of *Facienti quod in se est . . .* To help in the search for a solution, distinctions were introduced within the category of merit. Strict merit, or merit *de digno* or *de condigno*, gives an absolute right to reward. The early Scholastics unanimously denied that man can merit grace in this way. Merit broadly understood, or *de congruo*, gives an ability to receive grace which makes the gift of grace proper and therefore likely, though never strictly due. Most early Scholastics recognized this distinction and applied it to the interpretation of *Facienti quod in se est* . . . The person who does this merits grace.

With the great Scholastics of the thirteenth century, the same categories are used. And several attempts are made to reach deeper into the analysis of the *quod in se est* by which one may deserve grace *de congruo*. Generally speaking, the Franciscan authors taught both the absolute necessity of grace for justification and the achievement of moral good, and the normal possibility of preparing oneself to receive it. In the *Summa Alexandri,* a collective work containing texts of the founder of the Franciscan school, Alexander of Hales (c. 1185–1245) and his immediate followers, the one who does *quod in se est* obtains divine grace not by merit, but through God's pure liberality. This liberality is antecedent to grace. Yet there exists an innate capacity to know God, to pray, to ask for the good and even for faith. This capacity lies in *recta ratio,* the right reason. Nonetheless, it leaves man unworthy of grace *(indignus)*. God alone gives a sufficient disposition to receive his own grace.[68] That a divine assistance is required for such a disposition to grace leads Odo Rigaldus (d. 1275) to distinguish between "grace graciously given" *(gratia gratis data)* which, he believes, is offered to all, and justifying grace *(gratia gratum faciens)*. Only grace prepares for grace. Hence there must be two kinds of graces, of which the first prepares for the second. The first itself remains unprepared, even by a sinner's good actions; it is *gratis data,* graciously given. To the query "What can man do for salvation?" Odo would answer: By himself, nothing. But when, with the help of *gratis data* grace, one assents to *gratum faciens* grace, one does "what is in man." This, Odo calls "merit," but it is only congruent. Justifying grace is never due in strict justice, yet divine love will not refuse it to those who have been prepared for it—by God himself.[69]

The doctrine of Bonaventure (1217–1274) does not differ substantially from that of Odo. In keeping with the structure of Peter Lombard's *Sentences,* the tractate on grace in Bonaventure's Commentary follows that on *liberum arbitrium*. Bonaventure has already determined that *liberum arbitrium* is not only will, but intellect and will together;[70] that it has the ability to sin; that in the state of innocence our first parents had the capacity to resist temptation without a special assistance from God, though not without God's general influence; that we have now lost this capacity, because "our natural endowments, though they are substantially the same, are now diseased, wounded, and damaged."[71] The tractate occupies distinctions 26–29, being then followed by a discussion of original sin. While we cannot examine all the details, several points need to be mentioned. Bonaventure posits as necessary that grace *gratum faciens,* the grace of justification, adds something to the person who is now accepted by God. For in order to become acceptable, this person must receive a gift from God, which may be called an acceptability.[72] But is this acceptability other than the presence of Uncreated Grace—the Holy Spirit—or is a created grace placed in the person? At one point, Bonaventure admits that "faith and Scripture" require no more than Uncreated Grace, although he shares the common opinion "of the doctors of Paris" that there also is a created grace. Here he is concerned about Pelagianism and he finds this second opinion "more removed from the errors of Pelagius" because it implies a greater incapacity of man, which needs healing.[73] Much of his subsequent reflection studies the nature of this created gift. Let us note how Bonaventure formulates the purpose of this grace: it is given "to make man acceptable to God; and so that man may, through it, reach the one and supreme Good; and so that work proceeding from the *liberum arbitrium* be meritorious before God."[74] Through it "the soul has God, and God indwells the soul."[75]

Thus the notion of merit is again introduced into the discussion. Like his predecessor Odo, Bonaventure distinguished the two sorts, *de congruo* and *de digno,* also called, in the Commentary, *de condigno.* Condignity establishes a proportion of equality or equivalence between action and reward; and there is congruity when, in the absence of such a proportion, something has been done which makes reward appropriate, though not strictly due. Yet Bonaventure also envisions degrees between the two, a sort of scale of congruencies, when congruency is joined to some elements of condignity.[76] Nature never deserves grace, and justification is always unmerited. But grace can merit more grace, in congruency. And grace can merit the glory of heaven, in congruency insofar as grace is in us, in condignity in that it is from God.[77]

On this precise question, Bonaventure becomes clearer in his little *summa,* the *Breviloquium* (c. 1257). Here he lists three levels of created grace, which determine three levels of merit. First, by the gift of *gratia gratis data* (gratuitously given), the sinner can merit justification, "but only with congruent merit."[78] Second, the grace of justification *(gratia gratum faciens),* which renders one acceptable to, and therefore accepted by, God, can merit its own increase:

> For, since God alone is the fontal principle of his grace, he is, by way of infusing it, the sole principle of its increase, grace being its principle by way of merit and dignity, and *liberum arbitrium* its principle by way of cooperation and service, in that it cooperates with grace and makes its own what belongs to grace.[79]

This is now called merit of dignity *(meritum dignum).* Third, at its highest, grace merits its eternal complement and fullness, heavenly glory. This is merit of condignity. It results from the equivalence of this level of grace with glory.[80]

Bonaventure concludes that without the grace of justification, *gratia gratum faciens,* the *liberum arbitrium* can neither triumph over the devil nor fulfill all the commandments.[81] Furthermore, it cannot even arise from its sinful condition through "the sole gratuitous mercy of God which learns to remit our sins on account of the satisfaction which Christ willed to make to himself when he offered himself for us on the cross." This formulation Bonaventure attributes to "heretics." Those are presumably Pelagians, since Bonaventure's objection is that they do not take seriously enough the wound of nature caused by sin. This wound is such that man is unacceptable to God until it has been healed; and it cannot be healed unless some healing process has taken place. This process results from grace: "The infused *habitus* of grace contributes to healing of the disease and re-formation of the image." Thus grace is indispensable "not only as the gratuitous will of God or as the generous passion of Christ, but also as a *habitus* in the soul."[82]

There undoubtedly exists a tension, which Bonaventure does not seem to have perceived, between this strong anti-Pelagian affirmation of grace as a created *habitus* necessary to heal the wound of nature, and Bonaventure's previous admission that, as far as faith is concerned, Uncreated Grace suffices. This tension is never quite smoothed over. One can sense it in the discussion of what human power can do without grace *gratis data*. Such grace, Bonaventure assures us, is always given. Neither before nor after justification is one without it. To the semi-Pelagian question—though not identified, and presumably not known as such—Bonaventure answers negatively: Man cannot of himself prepare for justification. Only under the impact of grace *gratis data* does man "do what is in him," thus obtaining a congruent disposition for justification.[83] Yet Bonaventure lets in a wedge: some moral good can be achieved "with the sole cooperation of God without any gift of grace." Such cooperation exists in Bonaventure's conception of illumination and of the natural desire for good. Bonaventure maintains his anti-Pelagian principle: the resulting good "prepares neither for grace nor for glory." But the reason now given shows how narrow has become the gap between no-grace and grace: this good "is not oriented, but is only orientable, to the final end." The actual orientation comes from God through grace.[84] As one could say, the final keystone is placed by the divine Architect, but the framework seems to be there already without grace. Another way of putting it could be that Bonaventure's theology of grace tries, without entirely succeeding, to harmonize the theology of Augustine and pre-Pelagian theology.

By comparision with Anselm, however, Bonaventure is in progress regarding redemption. This is no longer the solution of a dilemma concerning justice.[85] Its mode belongs to the area of congruency, not of necessity, even when described in terms of satisfaction, for it is understood that God could have brought us salvation in other ways.[86] Justice simply becomes one of the four cardinal virtues which, under grace, affect and transform the potencies of the soul. It is "rectitude of will in relation to another." Its object is "to give everyone his rights."[87] Redemption itself is not a matter of rights. By God's entirely gratuitous will, grace makes men *gratos,* accepted. Such acceptance is both justification and the removal of sin. It is obtained by Christ's passion and resurrection which, as it were, function in a fourfold way, as merit, example, model, and symbol of acceptance by God.[88]

Bonaventure also relates grace to the structure of the soul. In the faculty psychology of his time, not only the substance of the soul but also the three faculties (memory, intellect, and will) need to be restored to the image of God lost by sin. Hence the distinction, which he does not make absolute, between grace, which restores the substance of the soul, and the theological virtues of hope, faith, and love, which restore respectively memory, the intellect, and the will.[89] There is a sense in which faith is primary; in another, love is primary. Yet, since they both come from grace, ultimate primacy lies with grace. One may admit, however, that Bonaventure's long developments on the theological virtues strengthen the impression that, despite his explicit intent, he cannot quite expel the quasi-Pelagian postulate that grace, although it is God's, also belongs to the soul in which it inheres. This at least is the risk taken by Bonaventure's way of fighting Pelagianism.

Our long treatment of Bonaventure will now allow us to go into lesser details regarding the other Scholastics. Thomas Aquinas (1224–1274), in his *Commentary on the Sentences,* stands quite far from strict Augustinianism. He openly interprets *facere quod in se est* as the action of the will cooperating with grace in view of its own perfection. And he justifies this cooperation by claiming that, were it otherwise, the will would be violently compelled to act "by an exterior agent." Since it is against the nature of the will to be compelled from the outside, there must be in it an independent cooperation.[90] Even before any grace, one may be doing good. Such good is not "a meritorious cause" of grace, yet it is a disposition for it.[91] Those who have such a disposition may be said "in a certain sense to merit grace *de congruo.*"[92] Thomas hesitates about the vocabulary, but not about the two distichs of his doctrine: there can be a preparation for grace which is itself without grace; there is no grace without human cooperation.

In the *Summa theologica,* however, his position has become quite different. The relevant section, known as I II *(prima secundae),* was written around 1269–1272. Here, grace and its preparation are related to each other on the pattern of form and matter in Aristotle's philosophy. As there is no form without matter's predisposition to receive it, so there is no justifying grace without a preparation. But form and matter, in philosophy, are proportional to each other. Thomas Aquinas, who fully accepts the Augustinian analysis of original sin, finds no proportion between our corrupted nature and divine grace. He is assisted, however, in identifying the preparation for grace by the Aristotelian principle that the ultimate disposition of matter for its form comes from the form itself. Accordingly, the gift of justifying grace conveys to the soul an ultimate disposition to receive this grace. "A certain preparation of man to have grace coincides with the infusion itself of grace." And further: "An agent of infinite power does not need a matter or a disposition of matter which would have been posed by the act of another cause. But it must, according to the conditions of what it will do, cause in it both the matter and the disposition corresponding to the form. Similarly, in order that God may infuse grace in a soul, no preparation is required which he himself does not make."[93] In other words, God himself adequately prepares man for the grace of justification as he gives this grace.

Yet Aquinas still recognizes the existence of occasional acts of grace before justification. These, which he now calls helps *(auxilia)*, correspond to Bonaventure's graces *gratis datae*. They require no preparation since they are not forms of the soul. They do not constitute a habitus; they are only momentary acts. Any remote self-preparation for justifying grace results from such helps from God. In this sense, "the good movement of free will by which someone is prepared to receive the gift of grace is an act of free will moved by God. . . . It is principally from God moving free will. . . ."[94] This motion is further identified as "a gratuitous help of God interiorly moving the soul, or inspiring the proposed good."[95] Thus Thomas Aquinas affirms that no good action can be remotely preparatory of justification unless it comes from a divine motion. In so doing, he renews Augustine's insight on the nature of true *libertas:* true liberty does not derive from human power, but from God. It is God who moves the free will. This is a roundabout way of saying that, without such a motion, the will is not really free, even in its uncompelled choices.

The use of merit language by Thomas Aquinas should not mislead us. Merit is, for him as for most of the Scholastics, congruent or condign. But, as he insists, merit is not from self; it is always from grace. "It is manifest that no one can merit the first grace for himself."[96] Were there previous merit, he also remarks, grace would not be gratuitous. In what may be an allusion to the Council of Orange's condemnation of semi-Pelagianism, he adds:

> If we presuppose, as the truth of faith has it, that the beginning
> of faith is in us as coming from God, then the very act of faith
> follows the first grace and therefore cannot merit the first grace.
> Man is therefore justified by faith, not as though man, by believ-
> ing, deserved justification, but because, when he is justified, he
> believes, for the movement of faith is required for justification.[97]

Admittedly, the movement of faith is paired with a movement of the
will. But this proceeds from a divine motion: God "so infuses the gift
of justifying grace that at the same time it moves the free will to
accept the gift of grace, in those who are capable of this movement."[98]
With this gift of justifying grace and this motion of the will, there is
a motion of the intellect, and this is faith: "God moves the soul of man,
turning it to himself. . . . The first turning to God is through faith."[99]

Logically, this conception of the motion of grace implies predestination, since God chooses those he will move to justification. Thomas
does not hesitate to affirm it: "It is manifest that predestination is the
ordering of some to eternal salvation, which exists in the divine mind.
The realization of this ordering is indeed passive in the predestined; it
is active in God."[100] There is no double predestination, for predestination is only to salvation. Yet predestination has an opposite, reprobation, which "includes the will to let someone fall into sin, and to
give the pain of damnation for this guilt."[101] Here the difference
between reprobation and predestination to evil seems more verbal than
real. But at least it shows that Thomas is far removed, at this point,
from any trace of Pelagianism. As to God's action, he is willing to
respect its mystery.

In the matter of predestination, the doctrine of John Duns Scotus
(1266–1308) is practically identical with that of St. Thomas. The
elect are predestined to glory and beatitude regardless of merit on
their part; and as a consequence they are provided with the necessary
means to escape the *massa damnata* of sinful humanity. The reprobate are left without such means of escape, but they are not predestined to anything.[102]

In other aspects of the doctrine of justification, however, Duns
Scotus is in sharp disagreement with Thomas Aquinas. The two theo-

logians do not focus their attention on the same point. The central question, for Thomas, has to do with *facere quod in se est:* How can one so act as to be prepared for the grace of justification? For the Scottish theologian, it has become: How are divine grace and free will compatible? In fact, John Duns Scotus does not seem to raise the problem of *Facienti quod in se est Deus non denegat gratiam.* There is a simple reason for this: in his perspective, there can be no *facere quod in se est* as a preparation for grace. The necessity of grace *gratis data* in order to do what is required to receive grace *gratum faciens* is removed, and this at three levels.

First, the Scotist conception of the will postulates that the will is always entirely free, totally unmoved by anything other than itself. "Nothing other than the will is the total cause of willing in the act of willing."[103] But if the will determines itself by itself alone, there can be no divine contribution to it outside of the general influence of God by which all creatures are preserved in being and enabled to function according to their nature. A special assistance so that man "does what is in him" is not only superfluous; it is an impossibility, since it would contradict the very nature of the will.

Second, analyzing the notion of grace, Scotus makes a point which apparently escaped his predecessors. Created grace, whether *gratis data* or *gratum faciens,* does not exist in itself. It exists only in a person, from the moment it is received and as long as it perdures. That grace is an accident and not a substance—in the Aristotelian sense of these terms—was generally admitted. But Scotus draws from this a striking conclusion:

> ... God-giving-me-grace is my-receiving-it, for God does not cause grace unless I receive it; therefore his causing grace for me is receiving it; therefore what he causes is receiving.[104]

Thus the gift of grace is not antecedent to its reception. There is nothing before the gift which anticipates upon it.

Third, grace is willed by God, and divine will is also, by definition, undetermined except by itself; it cannot be prompted by any antecedent action or merit on the part of creatures. Men do not deserve grace, but receive and accept it. They do not buy grace, which is always entirely free. But the freely given grace is freely received, and does not exist before this reception. Once given, grace merits its own increase and its heavenly fulfillment by condignity. Strictly speaking, there is no congruent merit for justifying grace, though Scotus speaks of God giving this grace congruently, when man has performed the acts of natural goodness.[105] In Scotus' conception of original sin, fallen man can do so; since he can do so of himself, there is no need for a grace *gratis data*. Scotus invokes here the axiom that will later be called Ockham's razor: *plura non sunt ponenda sine necessitate* (entities should not be multiplied without necessity).[106]

John Duns Scotus makes Pelagianism and semi-Pelagianism simply impossible, by removing the possibility of acts antecedent to grace having an influence on the giving of grace. Interpreters of Scotus are easily confused by the fact that congruent merit is reintroduced by Scotus in his discussion of the value of attrition as a disposition for forgiveness of sins. Here again, Scotus denies the need for special assistance, yet he maintains that "attrition . . . is a congruent disposition or merit for the removal of mortal sin."[107] Is Scotus inconsistent? I would rather think that he is not now researching intrinsic necessity, but investigating the system of salvation established by God, according to the distinction, made famous a little later by the Nominalists, of *potentia absoluta* and *potentia ordinata*. The question is: Does God want attrition to be a proper disposition for forgiveness? Scotus is therefore able both to accuse Thomas Aquinas and his followers of making God unjust (by giving to one a motion of the will which is denied to another), and yet to affirm the predestination of the elect as firmly as Thomas Aquinas, while leaving the reprobate entirely to themselves as the cause of their reprobation.[108] The relation of predestination to the acts of the elect remains mysterious; but this is so with all doctrines of predestination for which God not only foresees, but also foreordains.

The doctrine of grace takes a new turn in the later Middle Ages. Generally speaking, the Schoolmen now take their cue from Scotus' removal of the necessity of a special grace—*gratia gratis data, auxilium*—to prepare the reception of justifying grace. But they understand this point in another way than the subtle Doctor. William of Ockham (c. 1290–1349/50), the *venerabilis inceptor* of the theological movement known as Nominalism, envisages grace at two levels, in keeping with his fundamental distinction of two orders in the power of God, *potestas absoluta* and *potestas ordinata.* Absolutely speaking, there is no merit and no preparation for grace. In the actual dispensation chosen by God, however, God has committed himself to a certain sequence of actions: the gift of grace usually follows the doing of good actions. Like Scotus, Ockham makes self-determination the essence of will; and so free will is a pre-condition for both salvation and damnation. The human will chooses or rejects justification. In a sense, then, it is the agent of salvation, but only in the order of *potentia ordinata:* this is how God has freely decided that salvation should be given. In itself, *de potentia absoluta,* justifying grace is entirely and exclusively God's doing. Thus Pelagianism is rejected in principle, though at the practical level, in the normal order of things decreed by God's liberality, one's free acts contribute to the preparation for grace.

Later medieval theology, even among followers of Ockham, was itself divided on these matters. The strict Augustinian tradition was not lost. At Oxford Thomas Bradwardine (c. 1290–1349) defended the theology of Augustine in a special tractate against the new Pelagianism, *De causa Dei contra Pelagium.*[109] Above all, the Augustinian friar Gregory of Rimini (d. 1358), although a Nominalist in many aspects of his *Commentary on the Sentences,* espoused strict Augustinian positions concerning predestination, grace, and the will which is unfree without grace.

To whom did the last word, before the Reformation, belong? It has been widely held that influential theologians related to Nominalism, such as Robert Holcot (d. 1349), Peter d'Ailly (1350–1420), Jean Gerson (1363–1429), and Gabriel Biel (d. 1495), adopted Pelagian or quasi-Pelagian positions. Thus Heiko Oberman wrote: "It is evident that Biel's doctrine of justification is essentially Pelagian."[110] Yet the question is still debated. Other scholars hold for the exact opposite: when seen in the light of the fundamental distinction between God's *potentia absoluta* and *potentia ordinata,* Nominalist theology is consciously anti-Pelagian, since the entire order of *potentia ordinata* rests on the gracious will of God.[111]

The medieval debates on grace ended on the following dilemma: If justifying grace is congruently prepared by human nature, then grace, being in some sense merited, is not entirely gratuitous; but if grace is entirely gratuitous, then it is given to some and not to others regardless of merits or preparations, and the goodness of God is thrown in doubt, since some are then predestined to grace and salvation, and others are abandoned to sin. The choice appears to be between some form of Pelagianism and double predestination.

The solutions proposed by the Scholastics may be reduced to five:

1. The undeserved gift of justifying grace *(gratum faciens)* is prepared by those who "do what is in them" after receiving a preparatory grace *(gratis data)* which enables them to do so. This is the option of the earlier Franciscans and Bonaventure.

2. The underserved gift of justifying grace is given to those who, impelled by a gratuitous motion from God, have through their good will and actions done what is in them, thus preparing the "matter" which justifying grace needs to act in them as the "form" of their life in Christ. This is the option of Thomas Aquinas and his followers.

3. The undeserved gift of justifying grace is given without any merit to those who have been predestined for it out of the *massa damnata* of sinful humanity. This gift is denied to those who have been predestined to remain condemned. This is the strict Augustinianism of Gregory of Rimini.

4. The undeserved gift of justifying grace is given to those whose self-determining will receives, in a total and unique movement, this very gift of justifying grace. There are no preparatory graces; and purely natural preparations, such as a naturally good life, are entirely inadequate to ensure the consent of the will. This is the option of John Duns Scotus and his school. In any case, granted Scotus' principle that "willing the end must precede willing the means," the predestination of the elect is logically and ontologically anterior to the graces received in this life.[112]

5. It is Ockham's doctrine, endorsed by Biel, that God could have willed predestination either with or without previous merit, but that the ground for merit does not lie in man's actions, but in man's being accepted by God in view of his future predestination, before any merit of his own. In this case, the Nominalists are not Pelagian, and they deny that one can be saved *ex puris naturalibus,* without grace.

One may formulate at this point what would have been a Pelagian position: the gift of justifying grace can—by God's free decree—be deserved without divine assistance by human nature. By "doing what is in them," human persons merit grace as a reward. Ockham was accused of this as early as 1326 by a theological commission appointed by John XXII. Although his condemnation on this point was certainly erroneous, the Pelagian label has stuck to the whole Nominalist system in the average history of theology.

If such was the theological situation at the start of the sixteenth century, the total religious picture was more confused still. At the popular level, theological conceptions were undoubtedly contaminated by the vagaries of popular preaching and piety. At least the desire to earn merits through the system of indulgences which had come to be connected with the understanding and practice of the sacrament of penance tended to push practical Christianity and pastoral theology toward some form of Pelagianism, away from the central Catholic tradition in its Augustinian and semi-Augustinian forms. This is precisely what Luther opposed.

III.

THE THEOLOGY OF LUTHER

Few theologians have been, in Catholic history, more controversial than Martin Luther. No one has inspired on such a broad scale both enthusiastic following and passionate opposition. This was to a large extent Luther's own doing. Very effective as a polemicist, he also let himself be carried away into notable excesses of language. And while he could be a moving and persuasive spiritual author, he also enjoyed a natural boisterousness which could be as objectionable to his adversaries as it was at times embarrassing to his friends. Undoubtedly, some of his actions were not calculated to make his supporters comfortable. In 1525 Philip Melanchthon, complaining to a friend, bemoaned Luther's marriage: "You might be amazed that at this unfortunate time, when good and excellent men everywhere are in distress, he not only does not sympathize with them, but, as it seems, rather waxes wanton and diminishes his reputation just when Germany has special need of his judgment and authority."[1] Later, in 1540–41, many—though not Melanchthon—were appalled at Luther's approval of the bigamy of Philip of Hesse.[2] Largely on the basis of the less constructive episodes of Luther's stormy life Catholic authors in general have not been inclined to apply to him the principle of "empathetic evaluation,"[3] even when they have not fallen into the excesses of Cochlaeus.[4] Yet Luther's doctrine should not be judged on his ambiguous behavior at moments when he was sorely pressed and may not have lived up to his best insights. It is to be assessed for itself, preferably as he formulated it in his less polemical writings.

One of these is Luther's *Commentary on Galatians* of 1519. This is the fruit of his teaching at the University of Wittenberg, where his lectures on Galatians started in October 1516, following lectures on the Psalms and on the Epistle to the Romans. Already his *Commentary on Romans* contained the heart of his interpretation of Paul. The *Commentary on Romans,* however, exists only in the form of notes on selected passages. By contrast, the *Commentary on Galatians* is a continuous text going carefully over all the verses of the Epistle. It is clear, written in Luther's spontaneous and simple Latin, which is closer to that of the Scholastics than to that of the humanists. Luther particularly liked the Letter to the Galatians, on which he lectured again in 1531, these lectures being published, in 1535, in the form of a much longer commentary. Luther actually preferred his second commentary. Yet the twofold polemic which he led in it, against the Schwärmer and the Pope, makes its tone less serene and convincing. I will therefore begin with the earlier commentary before looking at the later one, and rather than follow Luther's text chapter by chapter, I will select a few themes.

Many expressions which will become standard and may be considered typical of Luther's theological emphasis are already used in this work. The Christian is *simul justus, simul peccator* (just and sinner). The opposition between Law and Gospel is sharply delineated. Justice is *sola fide* (by faith alone). Christian freedom is contrasted with human freedom. Luther does not recoil from what strikes the modern reader as hazardous allegories. Galatians 5:12 reminds him of Deuteronomy 23:1, where eunuchs are forbidden to enter the assembly of God. Luther comments: "The two testicles are certainly the two testaments. . . . Is not the female uterus the will and the conscience?" He adds: "But I omit these things, for the pure discover them by themselves, and the impure do not hear them without danger."[5]

At the time when the Commentary is printed Luther has started on his reforming career, but he still hopes that the reform will take place within the traditional institution of the Church. He is already under a cloud for his *Appeal to the Future Council* of November 28, 1518. Yet the papal bull *Exsurge Domine* has not been promulgated. It is precisely in 1519, at the Leipzig disputation, that Luther publicly formulates his conviction that one is not bound in conscience by the decisions of Councils. In the preface to his *Commentary on Galatians,* however, Luther affirms a doctrine on the papacy which is certainly orthodox by Catholic standards: "I hold in honor the Roman Pontiff and his decrees; no one is superior to him, and I see no exception to this but the Prince of this Vicar, Jesus Christ, our Lord and the Lord of all."[6] The Roman Pontiff is "the Supreme Pontiff." Luther rightly objects to the cardinals identifying themselves with the *Ecclesia Romana*. The Roman Church itself is a "fine copyist" whose task is to write down "faithfully" not only customs and traditions, but also Scriptures and reasons. Luther adds: "I make a long, wide, deep distinction between the Roman Church and the Roman curia. The former I know to be the most pure dwelling-place of Christ, the mother of churches, the mistress of the world, though in the spirit . . . the bride of Christ, the daughter of God. . . . The latter is known by its fruits. . . ."[7] Such a distinction of course is not unknown among Catholics today. In the case of Luther, these and other similar texts point to an important fact: his doctrine on justification was not developed against Roman teaching. It antedates the violent opposition to everything Roman that will merge from his condemnation by Leo X. There is therefore no *a priori* reason for those who still share Luther's earlier views of the Roman Church and its bishop to be suspicious of the heart of his teaching on faith and works.

"I most purely love, not only the Roman, but the whole Church of Christ." Luther is aware that he will be judged at the last day on his stand by "the truth," and that there must be reciprocity between the *pro nobis* of Christ's actions and the *pro Christo* of our own. "The word of God has never been preached without blood or danger. And as he died for us, so in turn he demands that we also die for him in confessing him; and the servant is no higher than the lord."[8] Christ died, not for nothing, but for us; not only for others, but also for me. "It will not help you to believe that Christ was given for the sins of other saints, and to doubt about your own sins."[9] In the background there stands the conviction, inherited from Luther's spiritual and theological mentor, St. Augustine, that "the virtues of pagans are but fallacies." The natural man belongs to the sinful world. It does not help at this point to indulge in metaphysical distinctions between the nature as such, which would be good, and the concrete reality of evil existence. When Scripture affirms, "Every man is a liar" (Ps 116:11), "it does not qualify him according to his substance, metaphysically (for thus theologians find nothing in man which is not worthy of praise), but theologically, as he is in the eyes of God."[10] Before the universal experience of evil, the remedy is not obedience to the law, whether that of the Old Testament or that of human societies. For no one has the capacity to obey the Law as it should be obeyed for salvation. As in his other works, both of this period and of later years, Luther is clear as to the scope of Christian obedience. In the famous phrase of his opusculum, *The Freedom of a Christian Man* (1520), "A Christian is a perfectly free lord of all, subject to no one. A Christian is a perfectly dutiful servant of all, subject to all."[11] A Christian obeys the laws, knowing that such obedience will not save. It is not a deserving work. In fact, it is not a work at all. It is rather an aspect of the way faith is lived out in concrete existence in human society, where both the Church and the secular powers have passed laws and imposed rules of order. Yet faith does not give such obedience the capacity to save or to acquire merits. Laws can be obeyed also by those who have no faith and those who are not saved. "The law preaches to do and not to do what should be done and not done, what has been done and not done, and even the impossible; and thus it ministers only the knowledge of sin."[12]

The remedy to the evil of human existence is not obedience, but, precisely, faith. Psalm 2:12 enjoins, us, as Luther explains it, "to follow the discipline, that is, to believe in Christ with pure faith, and to honor him. For faith is due to the truth which is nothing except God alone. So faith is the most true and interior worship."[13] Only by faith is the Gospel apprehended. The Gospel "is the doctrine of spirit and grace."[14] It preaches "that sins have been forgiven and all has been fulfilled and done,"[15] that is, by Jesus Christ. Thus the faith of Luther is entirely Christocentric. This is manifest in the teaching material to which Daniel Olivier has drawn attention.[16] It is also a central lesson of the *Commentary on Galatians,* a lesson for which Luther finds eloquent formulations:

> Everyone who believes in Christ is just, not yet in reality, but in hope. He has begun to be justified and saved. . . . In the meantime, while he is being justified and saved, whatever sin remains in his flesh is not imputed to him, on account of Christ who, as he is without sin, being already made one with his Christian, intercedes for him with the Father.[17]

Here as elsewhere, Luther sits loose on vocabulary. His methodology is more rhetorical than Scholastic. He is not chary of dialectical contrasts: one is "together, therefore, just and sinner,"[18] "sinner and non-sinner, fulfiller and non-fulfiller of the law."[19] As Luther also writes, "In Christ the justified are not sinners, and yet they are sinners."[20] He may pass from one problematic to another despite differences in their language and perspectives. Thus Luther opposes Law and Gospel. But he also says that there are two Laws, one of which is the Gospel. Using surprisingly modern language, he writes: "The Law of the letter and the Law of the spirit differ like signifier and signified, like word and reality."[21] And this Law of the spirit is beautifully described as being "written in no letters, proclaimed in no words, thought in no concepts"; rather, "it is the very living will and the experiential life, even the reality itself, which is inscribed in the hearts only by the finger of God."[22] This description already suggests the famous passage where, some sixty years later, St. John of the Cross will speak of "substantial locutions," by which God inscribes his communications in the Christian soul. Like Luther's Law of the spirit, this locution differs from spoken words, whether exterior ("successive locution" in John of the Cross' vocabulary) or interior ("formal locution").[23]

Just as Luther, without changing his basic conception, alludes to one Law and two Laws, he can speak of one justice and of two justices. There is indeed only one justice, that of Christ, since everything that comes from human initiative is sinful. Yet one may also say that two justices stand opposed to each other. There is first a justice of the works of the Law through which no one is justified before God: it is "a servile justice, mercenary, fictitious, specious, external, temporal, worldly, human,"[24] contributing nothing to the future life, although in this life and society it deserves rewards, glories, and honors. Another justice is "interior from faith, from grace";[25] by it those who despair of worldly justice "humbly confess themselves to be sinful." It is "no other than the invocation of the name of God," for this name is "mercy, truth, justice, strength, wisdom and accusation of one's own name."

It is indeed paradoxical, yet true, that the justice without which we are not alive in the Christian sense of the term is never ours. In a sermon of the same period as the Commentary, Luther calls it an "alien justice." It is alien because it is not ours, but Christ's. In this sermon, however, Luther sees it producing in us a second justice which is ours "not because we alone work it, but because we work with that first and alien righteousness."[26] While this shift of vocabulary may be confusing, the meaning is crystal-clear: this justice is ours as not ours, for it is Christ's. The effect of it is that our sins, though our very own, become, not ours, but Christ's: "The one who believes in Christ, and by the spirit of faith is made one with Christ, not only satisfies for all, but even acts in such a way that all things are due to him, for he has everything in common with Christ. His sins are no longer his, but Christ's."[27] In contrast with the justice of men and of the Law, this is indeed no less than "a new justice and a new definition of justice."[28] The justice of men is *ab extra,* from outside. It works and is manifested in the open, yet it comes from us and only from us. But the true justice is *ab intra ex fide:* it works inside, in a hidden way, and it comes from faith. Achieved by Christ, it is given to those who, despairing of themselves with their achievements and their works, rely totally and exclusively on Christ. "Christ alone, and not our reason, is the light and the life of men."[29] In later works Luther will often say that one justice is "passive," the other "active." Coming from Christ, the true justice is passively received in us. The false justice of the flesh is active: it is solely our own work.

As one can gather, Luther is flexible on the vocabulary as long as the Christocentric nature of justification is made clear. In his attempt to clarify the true doctrine, he even uses the very modern structural device of diagramming the two types of justices and their contrasted relationships. At the beginning of his Commentary on Chapter 5, Luther takes his clue from Romans 6:6–7, which he paraphrases with a diagram:

Let us put it in order and structure:
     liberty of justice   slavery of sin
     slavery of justice   liberty of sin.

Luther comments: "He who is free from sin is made the slave of justice. He who is the slave of sin is free from justice, and vice versa."[30]

This formulation is all the more remarkable as it corresponds perfectly with conjunction and disjunction in the analysis of signification which is current in contemporary structuralism. As Luther suggests, there is a vertical relationship of implication and presupposition between liberty and slavery in the order of justice. Those whose freedom comes from justice are also slaves to justice; their freedom is a service. And likewise those who are slaves of sin have also the false freedom that derives from sin. Luther could have mentioned two other dimensions of his quadrilateral. There is a diagonal relationship of contradiction between justice as true freedom and sin as false freedom, just as there is contradiction between justice as slavery (service) and sin as slavery. And there is also a horizontal relationship of inversion between the liberty of justice, which entails the slavery of justice, and the slavery of sin, which is brought about by the freedom of sin. In contemporary semiotics these dimensions are called the deixis, the schema, and the axis. In a previous study I have shown what part they play in theological methodology;[31] I have also drawn attention to their application to ecclesiastical structures.[32] Luther had presumably taken a hint from Aristotelian logic, where these semiotic developments are anticipated. His stroke of genius was to discover the applicability of such a dialectic to the heart of the Christian Gospel.

With Luther's concept of justice we are in fact at the center of a complex of implications, contradictions, inversions, which holds the key both to the personal experience of sin and grace in the faithful, and to the symbolism of the Christian Gospel and of Christian theology. The very concept and practice of symbolism as the two basic levels of the sacraments and of the speaking of the liberating word have to be understood in reference to this key. For it is in relation to the redemptive grace of Christ that sacraments have meaning and efficacy, and it is in relation to the word of God that the words of proclamation, pronounced by failing and mendacious humanity, are invested with sense. We are here at the very source of Christian semiotics: all communication and formulation of the Christian message witness to the transformation of sinner into saint. Elements belonging to this world are, in the sacraments, signifiers of divine grace. The human words of natural languages become in the kerygma—both in Scripture and in proclamation—the word of the Lord. The sinner is made, by Christ's justice, just.

The dialectic envisaged by Luther is not a psychological process. A psychological process would include preparation, stimulation, response, and follow-up. But there can be neither time sequence nor degrees in the justice which is of Christ. This is totally given through the Spirit at the moment chosen by God. It is to be understood theologically, as God's sovereign, immediate, and total act in Christ, not psychologically, as an unfolding of the human soul. Yet Luther is protected from the danger of perfectionism by his insistence on *simul peccator,* which balances the *simul justus.* As awareness of sin protects the saint from the temptation of pride, the *simul peccator* is a doctrinal necessity of the *simul justus.*

If indeed, by the very nature of grace, the divine gift is total and instantaneous, the way in which each person receives the gift and lives in keeping with it is successive, with the very successiveness of human life. The temporal condition of the life of grace is reflected in the *Commentary on Galatians.* On the one hand, the gift is total: "To clothe oneself with Christ is to clothe oneself with justice, truth, all grace, and the fullness of the law. . . . If you clothe yourself with Christ, and Christ is the Son of God, you too by this same clothing are children of God."[33] Nothing can break such a union: "Christ cannot be separated from us, nor we from him, since we are one with him and in him, as the members are one in and with their head."[34] On the other hand, the Christian life is a *transitus,* a passage. Such expressions as redemption, adoption, and filiation

> are not to be understood in such a way that they would be fulfilled in us, but that Christ has completed that by which they will be completed in us. Thus all is begun so that from day to day it is perfected more and more; therefore one speaks of the passover or passage of the Lord, and we are called Galileans, that is, migrants, for we have been redeemed from Egypt through the wilderness; that is, through the way of the cross and passion we have access to the promised land, we have been redeemed, and we are constantly being redeemed; we have received and we still receive the adoption; we have been made, we are, and we become children of God; the Spirit has been sent, is sent, and will be sent; we know and we shall know.[35]

Thus are we justified in Christ and sinful in ourselves. Therefore Luther can also say: "Thus we in the Church are indeed healed, yet we are not fully healthy. For this we are called flesh, for that we are called spirit. . . . All men are two, and the total man is one."[36] It is in hope that we are saved. "Everyone who believes in Christ is just, not yet fully in reality, but in hope. He has begun to be justified and healed."[37] Our inner unity is such that at the same time we are totally flesh and totally spirit. "The whole man is the spiritual man when tasting the things of God, he is the carnal man when tasting the things of self."[38] By divine graciousness, our sins are not imputed to us while we are still on the way, in transit. One cannot speak of a progress of grace and sanctification, since the divine gift is total and instantaneous. Yet we should think of ourselves as children who are being taught and led. "We must be spirit, yet we are still under guidance and, so to say, in the formation of our spirit."[39]

The ideal is simply to abandon oneself in the hands of God. Like some of the great saints of the Catholic mystical tradition, Luther pushes this abandonment to the point of total indifference to self. "The Christian or faithful," he writes in a striking formulation, "is a man without a name, without a face, without a distinctive mark, without a personality. . . . Where there is unity, there is neither face nor distinctive mark, not even a name. And for this reason the Church is called in the Scriptures latent and hidden."[40] Luther here has in mind both the presence of the Church in the world and the self-awareness of each of the faithful. This should be a holy indifference, since nothing can be claimed for myself and as mine, when I share everything in Jesus Christ: "In Christ all is common to all, all is one and one is all."[41] There is no more need for personal choice. The realm of Christian freedom is not that of human freedom. "There is human freedom when the laws change but not the people. There is Christian freedom when, the laws remaining the same, the people are changed. . . ."[42] The two freedoms do not function in the same manner: "We are not free from Law in a human way, by which the Law should be rescinded and changed, but in a divine and theological way, by which we are changed. . . ."[43]

This view of perfection throws light on the inherent danger of the classical expression, *facere quod in se est*. If we count on what we do, we are likely to become immune to the true knowledge of Christ as the only Savior. Luther rightly remarks: "Whether they do what is in them or not, all should despair of themselves and put their trust only in God."[44]

Luther's doctrine on justification in 1519 was in harmony with the dominant trend of the previous Catholic tradition as this had taken shape under the impact of Augustine. Against his immediate predecessors, the Nominalists, Luther asserted the sovereignty of grace and the human incapacity to contribute to one's salvation by "doing what is in oneself." Better than the great Scholastics, he avoided the pitfalls of "cooperation" as a category refering to human engagement in one's salvation.

Did Luther's intent and doctrine change later? In order to answer this question, we should read the *Commentary on Galatians* of 1535. Undoubtedly, this is harder reading for Catholics. The anti-Roman tone is much more marked, though it is not entirely negative, and it is balanced by equally sharp attacks against what modern authors often call the "left wing of the Reformation," the people whom Luther calls *phanatici* (the *Schwärmer* of this German writing). Luther is also more conscious than before of contradicting some frequent assumptions or positions of Scholastic theology regarding works, merit, charity, hope and, more basically perhaps, the very description of faith which is widely held by his Roman opponents. At the same time, the Commentary of 1535 is a profoundly moving and human document. The personal tone is pronounced; reminiscences from Luther's earlier life and testimonies from his own experience abound. Luther speaks of his spiritual life, in relation both to his early struggles with sin and Law and to his profound intimacy with Christ.

When Luther reads Galatians in 1531, the Augsburg Confession has been adopted by his supporters. And thus Luther may feel that his central view of justification is now securely held by a sizable portion of the Church. Luther has maintained his sacramental-eucharistic realism against Zwingli. His fight with the enthusiasts, which was exacerbated by the Peasants' War, has turned more theological than political. Luther is indeed at the high point of his theological powers. Calvin's sacramental theology is yet to challenge his own. His horizon has not yet been darkened by bickering among his supporters concerning the sacraments. Melanchthon's irenic mediation has not yet been proposed, even if one may suspect that, in Melanchthon's mind, the formulae of the Augsburg Confession and of the *Apology* (1531) may not entirely correspond to the full position of Luther.[45]

The Commentary of 1535, to this reader at least, conveys the impression that, whereas there is no difference in basic doctrine with that of 1519, the tone has changed. This is due, not so much to what

Luther now says, as to how he says it. As in 1519, the center of the
Commentary is justification by faith. But Luther is now more certain
of his method. The former Commentary antedated the Heidelberg disputation, when, in 1518, Luther began to formulate the theoretical
structure of his theological methodology. This is not the *fides quaerens
intellectum,* which, expressed by Anselm, had inspired the Scholastic
constructs. Such a search for the intellection of faith had led straight
to what Luther called a theology of glory. In line with some of the
pietist movements of the Middle Ages, Luther opted for a theology of
the cross. As he stated at the Heidelberg disputation, "The one who
beholds what is invisible of God through the perception of what is
made is not rightly called a theologian, but rather the one who perceives what is visible of God, God's 'backside' (Ex 33:23), by behold-
ing the sufferings and the cross."[46] The Heidelberg theses, however,
suggest a fundamental intuition; they do not propose a methodology.
The methodology had to be discovered by trial and error. And this
Luther had done through his many writings in the twelve years which
separated the Heidelberg disputation from the *Commentary on Galatians* delivered in 1531. He had had time to reflect, positively, on his
central view of justification by faith alone, on the opposition between
Law and Gospel, and on the idea of the two kingdoms; negatively, on
the incapacities of the classical Scholastic methods, on the shortcomings of humanists like Erasmus, Alberto Pio, and Henry VIII, and on
the mistakes of Zwingli's biblical humanism. His early interest in the
apophatic mysticism of the *Theologia germanica* had helped him to
perceive that true theology is not done at the level of *ratio* or even
intellectus.[47] *Ratio,* the rational faculty at work in human calculations
and schemes, is incapable of God; in Luther's words, it is "a whore,"
not indeed at its proper temporal level, but when it attempts to grasp
the spiritual and the divine. The sinfulness of the unfree will has a
parallel in the hybris of the human *ratio. Intellectus,* which furnished
the Scholastics with their instrument for theological speculation, is little better than *ratio,* for it trusts that intellectual work can lead to the
divine, thus tending to negate the Scholastics' own axiom that God is
"above all genus." True theology must be a matter of *intelligentia,* of
the high point of the soul. But, as Luther could learn from the mystical
movement represented by Meister Eckhart and the *Theologia germanica,* such a theology has to remain negative. It can only formulate

the conditions for knowing God. Such conditions include the denial of the human capacity to arrive at a knowledge of God as God is; such a knowledge is beyond human conceptualization and formulation.

Luther is therefore careful, in commenting on Galatians, to establish the proper parameters for theology. "One must carefully distinguish between philosophy and theology."[48] Positively, true theology is tied to the proper discernment of the Gospel: "The one who knows well how to discern the Gospel from the Law, let him give thanks to God and know that he is a theologian."[49] It contemplates the humiliations of the incarnate Word: "Christian and true theology, as I often insist, does not present God in majesty, as Moses and other doctrines have done, but Christ, born from the Virgin, our Mediator and Pontiff. . . ."[50] True theology does not know God as God is in himself, but as faith presents him:

> To give glory to God is to believe in him, to regard him as being truthful, wise, just, merciful, almighty; in sum, it is to acknowledge him as the author and giver of all good. This, reason does not do, but faith does. Faith perfects the Divinity and, so to say, creates the Divinity, not in the substance of God, but in us.[51]

We are indeed "outside reason" and "in divine theology" when "we hear the Gospel that Christ died for us and that, believing it, we are considered just, though sins, even grave ones, remain in us."[52] This is Luther's way of saying that theology takes place within faith. Therefore what is true of faith must be true of theology, and there is no theology unless it functions on the pattern of faith. There takes place a total reversal of value when, from nature and from philosophy with their works and their methods, one passes to theology. This is made clear in Luther's discussion of works. In nature, as Luther remarks, there must be a tree before there can be any fruits. In moral philosophy, good will and right method always precede action.[53] The dialectic of theology, however, is totally different. It follows the model of the incarnation: "In theology, faith is perpetually the divinity of works and is so present in the works as the Divinity in the humanity of Christ."[54] Faith is not only the starting point; it is the sum total of theology, as it is of the good works which follow faith in the Christian life. And thus Luther can say, in the Scholastic vocabulary which he does not hesitate to use when it serves to make a point:

> Theological work is faithful work. Thus is a theologian faithful, thus are right reason and good will faithful reason and will, when faith is universally the divinity of work, person, and members, the one cause of justification, which is later attributed to matter on account of form, to work on account of faith.[55]

Theology is therefore an experience rather than a task; it is an experience within faith. The formulation of this experience can only be made with common terms borrowed from ordinary life. But such terms must not be simply "transferred" to theology. They must become "clearly new." One needs "to rise higher." If indeed something becomes other than it is when it passes from its natural use to its moral-philosophical use, "much more does something, transferred from philosophy and law into theology, become other, so that it even has a new meaning, and it also demands right reason and good will, not morally but theologically. . . ." This is the newness of the Gospel, "that by the word of the Gospel I know and I believe that God has sent his Son into the world to redeem us from sin and death." Thus can Luther conclude: "In theology we have no other right reason and good will than faith."[56] If concepts, once totally transformed, have a place in theology, so do allegories, as long as they are used for illustration rather than demonstration: "Allegories do not provide firm proofs in theology, but, like images, they adorn and illustrate."[57]

Such an experiential theology is, like faith itself, "rather passive than active; that is, it is rather to be known than to know. Our action is to be passive under the God who works in us. . . . Thus our knowledge of God is merely passive."[58] But this passive state is the highest form of action and of thought. As Luther also says of those who believe: "They are like God, that is, they think of God in all things; as love is in the heart, they have the same form in their soul as God or Christ."[59]

It will be obvious to any practitioner of theology that these remarks do not fully determine what method should be used. They say nothing about the form of argumentation, the verification of theological statements, the value of demonstrations and conclusions. Luther does not aim at a new type of Scholasticism. He does better than that. He establishes the basis without which there can be no Christian theology. In the words I like to use to describe a theological method, he decides on a *focus* that will throw light on all theological assertions, by whatever way these may be arrived at.[60] It has been said that Luther makes justification by faith into a meta-linguistic principle by which to judge all theological formulations, or into a meta-theological principle by which to judge all theologies. I would rather say that, in the Commentary of 1535, justification by faith becomes a meta-methodological principle. *Meta* is employed here, not in the original Aristotelian sense of "that which comes after," but in the derived sense of "that which lies deeper." Deep within the systems of demonstration and verification which theologians favor, there must be an overall angle of vision, a *focus,* which Luther identifies with the experience of being justified by faith. This focus is Christocentric, since it is by and through Christ that we are justified. If this focus is kept constantly in view, it matters little to Luther where one looks for theological argumentation, since whatever is deficient in argumentation will be corrected by the experience of justification. We are therefore here at a central knot of all theology. We stand at a universal vantage-point which allows us to look critically at all theologies and to distinguish between what remains philosophical in theological speculations and what is true theology. Thus, meta-methodological means that all methodologies should at least be compatible with the experience of being justified, not by any good works of our own, but by faith in the one Mediator. The nearer this experience is to the focus of a theology, the closer this theology comes to what Luther would consider true theology.

The Commentary of 1535 not only formulates the basic principle of Luther's theology; it also applies this to the main aspects of justification. And here we see the meta-methodological principle functioning not only as a negative rule for theologizing (all theology should be compatible with it), but also as a positive rule, which directly organizes and structures all aspects of Luther's doctrine. This emerges from the critique which Luther makes of the Scholastic understanding of justification.

The opposition between Law and Gospel follows directly from Luther's basic principle. Since justification is the sovereign act of God who, through Jesus Christ, reconciles sinners to himself, it is for sinners the total expression of divine grace. There is no grace outside of it. Yet God's absolute sovereignty rules also over what is not grace. It rules then as Law. Law is the form taken for us by God's dominion over what is not his saving and reconciling grace. Thus Luther writes: "Whatever is not grace is Law. . . ."[61] Scholastic theologians, analyzing the structure of justification, include in it the sinner's actions, efforts, good intentions, and cooperative will. This is expressed in the axiom, *Facere quod in se est.* . . . But if man should "do what he can" in the natural or political realms, Luther cannot transfer this notion to "the spiritual realm, where man can do nothing but sin."[62] The Scholastics mingle grace and not-grace, grace and sin, in their accounts of faith, hope, and love. They make love *(caritas)* the form of faith, that which enables faith to be alive. But Luther, reversing the problematic, takes a dim view of love unless this is informed by faith: faith is the form of love. "Love, which suffers all, believes all, hopes all, also concedes, but not so faith. . . . By love the Christian concedes and tolerates all, and then is merely human."[63] The sovereignty over all virtues which the Scholastics attribute to love has now passed to faith. Faith is the form of all Christian behavior. Apart from it, love simply remains a natural inclination. When inserted in the spiritual realm, it becomes Law. "For if charity is the form of faith, I am immediately forced to believe that charity is the chief and greatest element in Christian religion . . . and I adhere to charity in order to love, and I come to morality."[64] But morality is Law. Luther can therefore conclude forcefully: "And thus I abandon Christ." His point of departure leads to relegating love to the domain of human action. Then, as he says it also, "charity tolerates all, cedes to all. On the contrary, faith tolerates nothing, cedes to no one. . . . In regard to salvation one must neither practice charity nor approve error."[65] There is a sense in which charity contradicts faith: "Faith trusts in God, and therefore it cannot be deceived; charity believes man, and therefore it is often deceived."[66] Taking one more step, Luther can then assert: "Charity may be neglected here without danger; not so the word and faith."[67] And he exclaims: "Accursed be the charity which is preserved through loss of the doctrine of faith."[68]

At this place, Luther is obviously not describing the Scholastic vision of *caritas:* being infused by divine grace in the human soul along with faith and hope, the Scholastic *caritas* is never merely human.[69]

Yet Luther's paradoxical language accurately exposes the Scholastic temptations of confusing merely natural love with infused *caritas,* and of making the love of natural man a condition for grace.

Meanwhile, Luther fully restores love in what is to him, in light of his focus on faith, the proper order in relation not to a "faith informed by love," but to a "faith which operates through love." The true *caritas* is informed by faith; it is posterior to faith; it is the fruit of faith. Not a virtue in Aristotle's sense, nor an inner strength or habitual behavior by which one would do good and merit grace, it is a relationship between those who have faith, their mutual support:

> The law of Christ is the law of love *(caritatis).* After Christ redeemed, renewed, and constituted us as his Church, he gave no other law than that of mutual love: John 13: "I give you a new commandment. . . ." To love *(diligere)* is not, however, as the sophists imagine, to wish good for another person; it is to bear another's burdens, that is, to bear what is painful to you and which you do not bear willingly.[70]

Such a love is rooted in faith, is inseparable from faith. Apart from it, faith is "abstract . . . vivid or simple"; with it, faith is "concrete . . . composite. . . ."[71] The works which flow from it must be seen "not morally, but theologically and faithfully."

As to hope, the third theological virtue of Scholastic theology, Luther treats it with great delicacy. Hope may be envisaged, Luther notes, in two ways: from the standpoint of its object, of what is hoped for, as in Colossians, and from that of its internal structure, orientation, or affection, as in Romans 8.[72] The object of hope is justification, for "our justice is not yet in reality, but is still in hope."[73] Hope is "a most sound and sweet consolation," by which I trust the promise that I have "a perfect and eternal justice."[74] Indeed, there is "a perfect justice prepared for me in heaven."[75] One perceives here the extrinsic nature of the final, heavenly gift, and already the intrinsic certainty that the gift is being given, though not fully, in the present life. Luther is therefore led to affirm both differences and a close relationship between faith and hope. "There is so great an affinity" between them "that hope cannot be torn from faith."[76] Luther, however, finds several levels of contrasts. Faith and hope differ by their ground in the soul (understanding—will), their office (knowing—exhorting), their object (truth—goodness), their order (beginning—continuation), their way of working (as teacher and judge—as fighter against all evils).[77] And he proposes highly suggestive models for their relationships. Faith and hope stand together on the pattern of dialectic and rhetoric, of prudence and strength, of intellect and will. The reference to dialectic-rhetoric is illuminating:

> Faith is the dialectic which conceives the notion of all the articles of belief; hope is the rhetoric which enlarges, urges, persuades, and exhorts to perseverance lest faith fall under temptation, so that it keeps the word and firmly adheres to it. Just as dialectic and rhetoric are distinctive arts, though so cognate that the one cannot be severed from the other . . . so faith and hope are distinctive qualities, yet faith is other than hope and hope other than faith, and yet because of their great mutual cohesion, they cannot be torn apart. As therefore dialectic and rhetoric mutually do business together, so faith and hope.[78]

This analysis of faith, love, and hope brings in its wake, as a necessary conclusion, the imputative character of the divine gift. For hope is grounded in the fact that "your justice is not to be seen, is not to be sensed, but it is hoped that it will be revealed in its time."[79] When Luther says that the works which faith operates through love must be seen "not morally but theologically and faithfully," he perceives a sharp contrast between the order of a natural morality, in which good works make a person good, and the order of theology and faith. Here, "Christians do not become just by doing what is just, but, being already justified by faith in Christ, they do what is just."[80] "For in theology those who have been made just do what is just; not so in philosophy, where those who do what is just are made just."[81] The extrinsic, or forensic, aspect of grace and justification follows as a matter of course. How are we justified? "First, through a remission of sins and an imputation of justice for the sake of faith in Christ; then through a gift and the Holy Spirit who begets new life, new motions in us, so that we formally fulfill even the Law. Whatever is not done is ignored for the sake of Christ. Then, whatever sin is left is not imputed to us."[82] As one can see, Luther uses both forensic and non-forensic language. For one may freely borrow terms from philosophy, such as "to do, to operate," and "transfer them to theology."[83] Once they are in theology, they take on a theological meaning, which is more properly expressed in forensic language. The justice which is given to us is not ours, for it is Christ's. Or, as Luther also writes, "Christian justice consists of two elements, faith in the heart and imputation by God."[84] The forensic language, which is more strongly marked now than in Luther's early works, wants to guarantee that the justice which is given to us by faith is indeed the justice of Christ:

> Christian justice should be properly and accurately defined as trust (*fiducia*) in the Son of God, or trust of the heart in God through Christ. Here one should add this specific note: this faith is imputed as justice for the sake of Christ. These two elements, as I have said, make Christian justice perfect: one, faith (*fides*) itself in the heart, which is a gift divinely given and formally believes in God; the other, that God considers this imperfect faith to be perfect faith for the sake of Christ, his Son, who suffered for the sins of the world, in whom I have begun to believe. And for the sake of this faith in Christ, God does not see the sin which is still left in me. . . . And imputation does this for the sake of the faith by which I have begun to apprehend Christ, for which sake God considers imperfect justice to be perfect justice, and sin not to be sin although it is truly sin. Thus we live under the veil of the flesh of Christ (Heb 10).[85]

As such a text eloquently shows, Luther's intent is, from the standpoint of the Christocentric character of grace and justification, unimpeachable. It undoubtedly implies a sharp critique of the Scholastic treatise on grace. Given his focus and his method, Luther has no choice but to condemn the congruent merit which Scholastic theologians interposed between human sin and divine grace. The Scholastic logic had created an entity which was ours only because given to us (the merit) and could not by itself fully do what merit is supposed to do (congruent). Luther's logic applied Ockham's razor to this concept, which seemed to be superfluous if faith and all its consequences were really and totally rooted in Christ. Luther's temperament and liking for colorful language then led him to express this critique in strong terms which were bound to shock and antagonize the followers of Scholasticism, as when he said that the doctrine of *de congruo* merit is "the theology of the anti-Christian kingdom."[86] At least before the Council of Trent, however, it would seem that his theology presented an acceptable alternative to Scholasticism, all the more so as no Scholastic explanation of grace had ever been quite unanimous, there being significant divergences among the Schoolmen.

Undoubtedly, Luther's approach presented a dilemma to his Catholic critics. Part of the responsibility for this falls on Erasmus' defense of free will, which led many among the Catholic polemicists to misunderstand Luther's view of the bondage of the will.[87] But, at a deeper level, forensic justification and the imputation of the justice of Christ were commonly taken by the theologians of the Counter-Reformation to contradict the reality of divine grace. They conveyed the impression to Luther's Catholic readers that justification is purely nominal, that it does not result in a transformation, an adoption, a filiation, and an indwelling of the three Persons, and that the good works inspired by faith are superfluous. This was the exact opposite of Luther's intent, whether in 1519 or in 1535. But theologians formed in the Scholastic tradition could hardly understand a perspective that was so new to them. Yet if Luther's language was new in relation to Scholasticism, it was closer to the problematics of Augustine and Paul. Unfortunately the Catholic mistrust of new formulations made Luther's critics miss the mystical depth of the reformer's theology of faith and its kinship with the apophatism of the Greek tradition and the stress of many Western mystics on the night of faith. As Luther had written in the Commentary of 1519:

> The Christian faith is not an idle quality . . . which could exist in mortal sin until love arrives and vivifies it; but if it is true faith it is a certain sure trust of the heart and firm assent, in which Christ is apprehended, so that Christ is the object of faith, though not really an object but, so to say, Christ is present in faith itself. Faith is therefore a certain knowledge or darkness which sees nothing, and yet in this darkness Christ, apprehended in faith, sits, as God at the Sinai and in the temple sat in the midst of darkness.[88]

The theology of Luther did not become simply the theology of the Reformation. It is true that John Calvin, who did not employ

Luther's theological method, endorsed his central conception on justification by faith alone, notably in the *Institutes,* III, Chapter 11. Yet when one looks more closely at the matter, it appears that Calvin has also modified the dialectics of Law and Gospel, with the introduction of what is known in Lutheran theology as the third use of the Law. The Law is not only for exhortation and condemnation (first use) and to bring sinners to fear punishment (second use), but also for the progressive sanctification of Christians (third use). Calvin explicitly mentions these three uses.[89] He also writes: "The Law was divinely given to us in order to teach us perfect justice; no other justice is taught in it than that which is demanded according to the decree of the divine will."[90] It exists "in order that human life be shaped in the Law, not only for external honesty, but for interior and spiritual justice."[91] There is therefore in Christian life a positive use of the Law which is instrumental in sanctification. This is tied to Calvin's view that grace is twofold. Grace is received only through faith in Jesus Christ and participation in him. But it is also diversified. The grace of justification derives from our being reconciled with God by Christ's work; the grace of sanctification or regeneration comes from his Holy Spirit, "to meditate about holiness and innocence of life."[92]

In Anglicanism, Luther's theology of justification has never been much at home. For one thing, Thomas Cranmer (1489–1555) was more Calvinist than Lutheran. For another, Richard Hooker (1554–1600), the great theologian of the Elizabethan period, struck out on his own. He could speak of "that grand question which hangeth in controversy between us and the Church of Rome, about the matter of justifying righteousness." But he also judged "the opinion of the Lutherans" to be "damnable."[93] Hooker took his distance from both Luther and the Council of Trent by leaning to a concept of double righteousness:

> There are two kinds of Christian righteousness: the one without us, which we have by imputation; the other in us, which consists of faith, hope, charity, and other Christian virtues. . . . God giveth both the one justice and the other: the one by accepting us for righteousness in Christ; the other by working Christian righteousness in us.[94]

Such a view was not far from that of the Regensburg Book, which had been rejected both by Luther and by the Roman leadership. By and large, however, the Caroline divines did not follow Hooker on this point.

As to the Puritan wing of the Church of England—which was later to form the bulk of English Presbyterianism—it came close to the formulas endorsed by Dutch Calvinists at the Synod of Dort (1617–1618). These were directed against the Pelagianism of the Arminians or Remonstrants, and they constituted an extreme reaction going far to the right of Calvin's own theology. The Synod of Dort adopted five articles, which taught unconditional election, limited atonement, the total depravity of man, the irresistibility of grace, and the final perseverance of the saints. At least the first four of these neglect some important nuances of Calvin's doctrine. The five Anglican delegates sent to Dort by King James I, who was attempting to exercise an international influence in theology, seem to have approved this ultra-Calvinism. Among them was the future bishop of Exeter and Norwich, Joseph Hall (1574–1656).[95] In spite of this, the Caroline divines did not share the positions of the Synod of Dort. In fact, they did not regard justification as a major point of divergence between themselves and Rome, even though they frequently argued against the notion of merit which they attributed to Roman theology.

The chief opposition, in Protestantism, to both Luther and Calvin, was to come from John Wesley (1703–1790), who, nurtured in High Church Anglicanism, became the initiator and guide of the Methodist movement.

IV.

POST-REFORMATION THEOLOGY

The decree of the Council of Trent on justification, promulgated in 1547, aimed at both the antinomianism of the *Schwärmer* and some aspects of the doctrines of Luther and Calvin. Yet the work of the Council was not negative. The Tridentine Fathers attempted a positive reconstruction of the Scholastic doctrine of grace in the light of the Reformation discussions, which incorporated some of Luther's basic concerns.

In the following pages I will try to indicate the essentials of post-Reformation controversies touching justification. I will focus attention, first, on the Council of Trent and its sequels, and, second, on the doctrine of John Wesley.

The Catholic theologians who rejected Luther's doctrine on justification were not entirely agreed among themselves, since diverse medieval schools continued to have adherents in the universities and the religious orders. Yet the adversaries of Luther could find a common point of agreement, albeit a negative one, in that they were all taken by surprise by Luther's theological method. Beginning, with the Scholastics, with an intellectual and spiritual tradition handed on from the Fathers through the mediation of the Schoolmen, or, with the Renaissance, from a reading of the Greek Scriptures in the light of the Catholic experience, they were at a loss to grasp a theological reflection starting at the experiential point where Christians, while united to Christ by grace, know themselves to be sinful in God's eyes. What had hitherto been treated as an incidental happening in the process of being justified by grace was placed at the very focus of Christian experience and the norm of theological reflection, not only for the question of justification but for all theology. Faced with this radical methodological shift, differences dwindled into insignificance, among the Scholastic theoreticians of grace and free will, between the "ancient" of the thirteenth century and the "modern" of the fourteenth and fifteenth. Though widely divergent, the Franciscan, the Thomist, and the Nominalist lines of thought, the humanistic scripturalism of Erasmus, and the theological compromise of double righteousness attempted at Regensburg in 1542[1] were equally challenged by a return to the one source, grace itself as received in the sinful human heart. No one among Luther's adversaries seemed to realize that, beyond differences in wording and points of view, they were struggling, not with a new theory or a new vocabulary, but with the most specific reality of the Christian experience, with what precisely was the Christian experience of grace as such.

This needs to be kept in mind as we read the decree on justification adopted at the sixth session of the Council of Trent, in January 1547.[2] It is difficult to appreciate the Tridentine Fathers' handling of the matter if one does not realize that they were not functioning at the religious depth of Luther's central concerns. Whatever shortcomings Luther had inherited from Nominalism he had largely overcome through his appeal to the basic experience of grace. But the personalities involved at Trent were little prepared by their formation and by the mood of the period to pay attention to this aspect of Luther's method. The Council of Trent restated therefore the Catholic notion of faith with two basic ideas in mind. On the one hand, the place of faith in the scheme of salvation had to be shown over against what was taken to be Luther's notion of justification by faith alone. On the other, the traditional doctrine had to be distinguished from what the Council took to be Luther's identification of faith (*fides*) with trust (*fiducia*).

The Tridentine decree comprises sixteen chapters and thirty-three canons or anathemas. The chapters being in the positive or affirmative mode and the canons in the negative mode, one should regard the sixteen chapters as explaining the Catholic doctrine, while the canons draw some conclusions regarding the formulations rejected by the Council. Yet these rejections or condemnations may not always apply in fact to what was effectively taught by Luther or Calvin, since the bishops and their theologians may not have been fully acquainted with, or may not have understood, the exact teaching of the reformers.

The first four chapters of the decree are introductory. In largely biblical language they describe the situation of the human race in relation to the sin of Adam (chapter 1), the advent of Christ, who came for the redemption of both Jews and Gentiles as a propitiation for their sins (chapter 2), and the necessity of being reborn in Christ by grace through the merit of his passion in order to obtain redemption and forgiveness of sin (chapter 3). Chapter 4 proposes a first description of justification as a passage *(translatio)* from the state of the sin of Adam to the state of grace and filial adoption through the second Adam, Jesus Christ; it points out that this does not take place without baptism or the desire thereof.

So far there is no difference between the Catholic and the Reformation teaching. The Council strikes a path of its own, however, in the next chapters. Before looking at the causes and nature of justification in chapter 7, the Council devotes chapters 5 and 6 to its preparation. Such a preparation is, in the case of adult converts, "necessary." The key to the conciliar doctrine is provided by the idea that faith is not the whole of justification, but only its preparation (chapter 6). While it is indeed possessed in seminal form with grace (chapter 7), justification does not become definitive before one dies, when it crowns the final perseverance of the saints (chapter 13). This place of justification in the schema of redemption is described with precision:

> . . . urged and assisted by God's grace, conceiving faith by hearing, they [the converts] are freely moved toward God, believing as true what has been divinely revealed and promised . . . (chapter 6) .[3]

Five elements in this sentence bear on the structure of faith:

- Faith results from the divine assistance; it is not man-made.
- It is occasioned by the preaching of the Gospel.
- It is free, in the two senses that it can be refused, and that we are moved by it into freedom.
- Its final aim is God himself.

- Its immediate object is the acceptance of revealed truths and promises.

One may sum this up in three antinomies. Faith is both free and gratuitous. It is both interior and exterior, receiving its immediate object from outside. Its object is twofold: ultimately, it is a divine action; immediately, it is a set of doctrines. The first antinomy belongs to the metaphysical order, the second to the logical, the third to the psychological.

Compared with the teaching of the Council of Orange, the first antinomy stands out. Trent insists on God's action, described in a way which is reminiscent of Orange: " . . . when God touches the human heart through an illumination of the Holy Spirit, neither is man *(homo)* himself doing nothing, as he receives this illumination which he can reject, nor can he of his own free will without the grace of God move himself toward being just in God's eyes . . . " (chapter 5).[4] Compared with the teaching of Luther, however, the third antinomy stands out. The Council is concerned, among other things, with the phenomenology of conversion, which was of no interest to Luther. In this we find one of the basic reasons for misunderstandings, but also the possibility of convergence, between Catholics and Lutherans, if at least the Tridentine phenomenology is not incompatible with Luther's focus on the immediacy of the divine action in the soul.

When Luther formulated his doctrine of justification by faith, he did not make faith a condition, or even the condition, for justification. Justification is unconditional. Faith was related, not to justification in the abstract and in general, but to the believer's own justification, to justification as it is lived out in our personal experience as Christians. While, contrary to some later Protestant developments, he did not eliminate the noetic content of faith, the content became inseparable from the subject's assimilation of faith. I believe that God gratuitously looks at me through the justice which is that of Jesus Christ. When I believe, I therefore know myself to be justified. Hence the difficult question of faith as trust, of *fiducia*.

One methodological point seems to stand out in the two problematics that we are examining. Once faith has been defined, at least in a provisional way, as the beginning of justification, then it follows that faith needs to be distinguished from, and therefore connumerated with, the other elements that may contribute to justification. Only in common with some other factors, that still need to be identified, does faith channel justification to us. Knowledge alone does not save. It can even be dead. One can of course wonder if a faith that is dead may be properly called faith. For Trent, faith can coincide with the abnormal situation of being without the indwelling of God in oneself. But such a faith does not save. It is only a belief without trust and without self-abandonment in the hands of God. However, the Council does not imply that this can be, either the first moment of faith, when we come to believe, or its last moment, when we leave the present life. It does imply that one can cease belonging among the friends of God without thereby rejecting the truth or the truths of faith. On this point it would seem that Trent marks a development over the Council of Orange. For Orange, the origin and the growth of faith require the gift of the Holy Spirit, the indwelling of God, as a spiritual-ontological requirement. Trent now shifts the question to the psychology of sin: grave sinners can remain believers. This point of view was of course in keeping with the medieval practice of the sacrament of penance.

Some sections of the Tridentine decree may convey the impression that the Council has adopted the schema of Thomas Aquinas concerning *de congruo* merit being prompted by an interior instinct of the Holy Spirit. Expressions of St. Thomas are indeed used, such as *vocatio, illuminatio,* and *inspiratio,* but they belong to the common vocabulary of the Schools. The Council is also compatible with what would seem to be Bonaventurian positions: it neither denies that good works may precede grace without contributing to conversion and salvation, nor rules out the schema of Duns Scotus, for whom the general influence of divine providence renders superfluous the interior instinct of St. Thomas. In other words, the Council does not wish to take sides among various Catholic schools of thought on grace and its preparation. What it rejects is the semi-Pelagian and Nominalist possibility of disposition for, or meritorious preparation of, conversion without the transitory divine grace called *gratis data* by the Scholastics. Faced with the multiplicity of medieval theories on the point, Luther had simply and neatly used Ockham's razor, eliminating everything in the human person and life that would seem to duplicate, even in a non-meritorious way, the work of grace. Faced with the same multiplicity,

Trent allowed the theories to co-exist, as long as the primacy of grace, along the lines of the Council of Orange, was preserved.

Another point needs to be made. For there is more, in the Council's identification of faith as the initiation of justification, than the start of a process of spiritual growth. Chapter 6 enumerates successive stages in the preparation to conversion: faith, fear of divine justice, hope in divine mercy, incipient love for God, regret for sins, desire for baptism. Here, faith constitutes the initial stage of a positive preparation for conversion. In Scholastic language, it would be the first phase in building up a *de congruo* merit that will allow us to "do what is in us." Such a faith, in the mind of the Council, is explicit faith in Christ. Thus, whatever natural movement may have preceded faith in the believer's concrete experience, it is faith alone which allows us to posit acts with a saving dimension. Before the beginning of faith, good actions, whatever else they may be in themselves, are non-meritorious and non-preparatory of salvation or conversion. In other words, explicit faith in Christ works a total change in the preparation of justification. It is a turning point which orients a person toward the fruits of faith, the chief of which is total conversion of the self to God under the impact of infused, sanctifying grace. But if this is the case, then one faces the logical paradox that it is faith which prepares faith. Where some later theologians of the Counter-Reformation will imagine that there may be two kinds of faith—an ecclesiastical faith leading to divine faith[5]—the Council rests on the paradox: faith comes from faith. The six steps mentioned—from faith to baptism and the new life of obedience, through fear of God, hope in God, love for God, regret for sins, desire for baptism—are not, as they may appear to be at first sight, successive. They all belong to the rich content of the act of faith, which is at the same time the beginning and the end of conversion, and also of whatever spiritual attitudes one may conceive between the beginning and the end. The process language of the Council of Trent is in fact not unlike the following passage from Luther's *Commentary on Galatians* of 1519:

And thus do not imagine that the life of a Christian is rest and quiet; it is rather a transit and a progress from vices to virtue,

from light to light, from virtue to virtue, and if someone is not in
transit, do not think that that is a Christian. . . .[6]

One should therefore conclude that both Luther and Trent affirm the
sufficiency and the necessity of faith apart from works, although with
different conceptualizations. And the Council has some infelicities and
inconsistencies of language, which precisely have been a source of confusion and misunderstanding.

Describing what justification is in itself, Trent underlines its positive side. It is not only forgiveness of sins, "but also sanctification and
renovation of the interior man *(hominis)* by a free reception of grace
and its gifts, by which man *(homo)* from unjust is made just and from
enemy friend. . . . " The causes of justification are detailed according
to a modified Aristotelian schema of the four causalities. But this
recourse to philosophical language is self-correcting, for all the causes
of justification are centered on God and Christ. The final cause relates
to God the Father, the efficient cause to the Holy Spirit, the meritorious cause to the incarnate Son, the instrumental cause to baptism.
Above all, "the only formal cause is 'the justice of God, not that by
which he is just, but that by which he justifies us,'" thus renewing our
spirit so that we are really, and not only nominally, just.[7] This is traditional teaching. It differs somewhat in words, but not truly in substance, from Luther's understanding of justification as making the sinner just.

On whether impiety and piety, injustice and justice, sin and holiness, co-exist in the saints, the one coming from the human person,
the other from divine grace, the Council of Trent remains ambiguous
where Luther is clear. Two readings are in fact possible. One may see
the two extreme moments in the conciliar formulation, sin and justice,
as separated by a time lag so that one would be made just only *after*
forgiveness has taken away sin. Yet the texts may also be read as
describing a permanent tension in the Christian heart, caught between
the human sinfulness which is its own and the divine righteousness
which comes by grace. In this second reading the Council does not
outline a history; it depicts a state. It does not itemize a process or a
progress; it rather exemplifies the situation and struggle of faithful
life. As the Tridentine decree states it, it is "in justification itself that
together with forgiveness of sins man *(homo)* receives all these infused

gifts through Jesus Christ in whom he is inserted: faith, hope, and love."[8]

Misunderstandings have indeed derived from the connumeration by Trent, following the Scholastic theologians, of hope and love with faith. In the perspective of Trent, faith without hope and love provides acquaintance with salvation and revelation without warming the heart or inducing the believer to total commitment. Such a faith is dead; it is nothing for justification (chapter 7).[9] By contrast with this faith without hope, the Council attributes to its adversaries a hope without faith. Hence its strictures against "the empty trust of the heretics" (chapter 9).[10] But of course the believer who shares Luther's sense of faith does not in fact rely on an empty trust, since the ties between faith and grace are central to Luther. Then, if we are conscious of our faith, are we not also conscious of saving grace in us? But the believer whose faith-knowledge, or belief, does not include hope and love denies to his faith the certainty of salvation. For otherwise justification would be a matter of the head, not of the heart; it would be a gnosis without a transformation of the whole self. If faith believes a divine promise, it implies also hope, but justification need not become conscious as long as we live in hope. In the Tridentine perspective, therefore, our earthly pilgrimage would seem to exclude the certainty claimed for justification by Luther.

Yet the Council did take some steps in Luther's direction. It asserted that by faith we believe "what God has revealed and promised, and first of all that God justifies the sinner through grace . . ." (chapter 6).[11] To the extent that believers know themselves as sinners, they also know that they receive the saving grace of God. Justification in Jesus Christ is then inseparable from faith. We believe that our redemption is in Christ Jesus. And this is no abstract idea, but a concrete experiential reality. Yet the Council does not admit that this faith includes the certainty of one's own justification (chapter 9). In the first place, Trent is chary of encouraging moral laxity through a mistaken assurance of personal salvation. In the second, it cannot see how the actual redemption of specific individuals could belong to the objectively revealed datum which constitutes the object of faith. Yet this position of the Council of Trent need not rule out that a practical certainty of being justified may also result from the experience of faith. If faith is the beginning of justification, beginning entails future growth. If faith is also the foundation and the root, the necessary condition of salvation (chapter 8), it is not sufficient in itself. The good works inspired by faith contribute to its growth (chapter 11).

Commendable as it is, this Tridentine concern to encourage and nurture the commitment of faith to a morally good life contains an unfortunate ambiguity. This is the notion that mortal sin, which excludes grace and justification, does not necessarily exclude faith (chapter 15). Such a sin obviously excludes living faith, but not statutory belief. At this point, Trent wavers between two concepts of faith: faith as living, and faith as statutory belief. Since a faith that is not living does not deepen or sharpen religious attitudes (canon 28), the situation of a believer who remains dominated by sin is both abnormal and unstable. Yet it would have been better to take Luther's hint and reserve the term "faith" for living faith.

The Tridentine position on the consciousness of justification has strict limits: faith does not bear on my own justification. Whether I am now justified or not is not revealed and cannot be, in the Tridentine sense, the object of my faith. The Council goes no further than this. It would still be faithful to Trent to esteem that the practice of faith can entail an experience of God which connotes an awareness of being justified. Scotist theology, which was represented among the bishops and theologians of Trent, inclined to such a view, and was by no means ruled out by the texts of the Council.

The remaining chapters of the decree logically follow from the distinction of faith from hope and love, of knowledge in the mind from the vital renovation of the person. There is progress in justification within the Christian life, and this progress is connected with growth in faith, hope and love (chapter 10). Justification frees us for the practice of the Commandments, a practice which is both necessary and possible (chapter 11). No one can boast of being certain of predestination (chapter 12), but final perseverance is another gift than that of faith (chapter 13). The faithful who sin have access to forgiveness in the sacrament of penance through the merit of Christ (chapter 14). Mortal sin takes away grace but not necessarily faith, in the narrow, intellectual sense of belief (chapter 15). As a result of justification, one may speak of the merits of the saints: these are the fruits of our union with Christ. "Thus it is not taught that we have a justice of our own as though it were from ourselves, nor is the justice of God ignored or repudiated; but the justice which is called ours because we are justified by it as it inheres in us is the very justice of God, since it is introduced into us by God through the merit of Christ" (chapter 16).[12]

In all these chapters, the Council follows the logic of its definition of faith in chapter 7. The clash with Luther's conceptualization, which is most clear in regard to the preparation and the follow-up of justification, flows chiefly from the ambiguity of the conciliar concern for both living faith and intellectual belief. Yet this collision could easily have been avoided. For chapter 8 recognized also faith in the more basic sense given to it by Paul:

> When the apostle says that man *(hominem)* is justified by faith and is justified freely, these words are to be understood as the perpetual consensus that the Catholic Church has held and expressed, namely, that we are said to be justified by faith because faith is the beginning of human salvation, the foundation and root of all justification, "without which it is impossible to please God" (Heb 11:6) and to reach the gathering of his children. We are said to be freely justified by God, because nothing of what preceded justification, be it faith or works, produces the grace of justification; "if it is grace, then it is not from works; otherwise (as the apostle himself says it) grace is not grace" (Rom 11:6) (chapter 8).[13]

In outlining the teaching of Paul, the Council of Trent was taking a step in the direction of Luther. Had the Council also emphasized that one is always at the beginning, that the greatest saint is also the greatest sinner, and that the fruits of justification are implicitly given in justification itself, then the difference with Luther would have remained minimal. Had chapter 8 with its more integral notion of faith, rather than chapter 7 with its narrower problematic, been taken as the basis for the rest of the decree, Luther's teaching could easily have become the official Catholic doctrine.[14]

The doctrine of the Council of Trent on justification may be regarded as a synthesis of the Thomist and the Franciscan orientations in the theology of grace. From Thomas Aquinas the Council inherited a primary concern for the primacy and supremacy of divine grace above all else; from the Franciscans, especially John Duns Scotus, it received a renewed concern for the integrity of human participation

JUSTIFICATION: AN ECUMENICAL STUDY / 80

in the process of salvation, a concern which echoed the pre-Augustinian emphasis and was germane to the Greek problematic. The danger of semi-Pelagianism was avoided, it would seem, for good. Having brought into one the two main schools of thought of the Catholic Middle Ages, the Council obtained what had been missing since the beginning of the fifth century, namely, the unanimity of Catholic thought on the nature of grace and the structure of its effects in the Christian soul. This was no small achievement. Yet it was done at the cost of refusing an alternative which was no less Augustinian than that of Trent, the theology of Martin Luther, even though the line between the two was perhaps more marked in the formulas than in the deep structures of what was meant. Yet this unanimity did not last. It was in fact broken quite early in the Counter-Reformation, and this at two levels.

As regards human cooperation with grace, two theologies were at each other's throat by the end of the sixteenth century. Following Luis Molina (1536–1600), many Jesuits held that human merit is logically antecedent to the decree of eternal predestination, which is therefore decided upon by God after (in logical, not chronological sequence) God has taken cognizance of what human liberty would do with or without grace (the *scientia media* of God; predestination *post praevisa merita*). Meanwhile, many Dominicans, in the wake of Dominic Bañez (1528–1604), considered that no good or meritorious act can be posited without one being moved by a "physical pre-motion" through which prevenient grace from God activates human freedom; such grace must have been decreed in a predestination which is already definitive before any foresight of human merit *(ante praevisa merita)*. The ensuing debate, known as the controversy *de auxiliis* (over the divine helps), was ordered to end in 1607 by Pope Paul V, who forbade the protagonists to accuse each other of heresy. In 1611, publication of further books on this question was prohibited. In 1625 and 1641, under Pope Urban VIII, the penalty of automatic excommunication *(ipso facto)* was added to these prohibitions.[15]

Meanwhile, the Jansenist movement raised other quesions in a related area. The movement originated in an excessively strict reading of Augustine by Jansenius (1585–1638), bishop of Ypres, and in the ascetic spirituality of Jean Duvergier de Hauranne, abbot of St-Cyran (1581–1643). It found fuel in what it deemed to be laxity in the implications of Molinism in the areas of morality and of the direction of consciences. Along with progressive views relating to liturgical renewal and reading of the Bible in the vernacular by the laity, it promoted abstention from the sacraments because of even the best Christians' unworthiness, a restrictive view of redemption, effective for the elect only, a belief in double predestination, a conviction as to the small number of the elect, and a renewed regard for good works and ascetic renunciation. While limiting the power of the bishop of Rome to matters of discipline and of doctrine over against matters of fact, the Jansenists upheld the Council of Trent, belonged squarely within the Counter-Reformation, and intentionally opposed Protestantism in all its forms. Their doctrines on grace incurred a series of Roman condemnations, from 1653 (condemnation of five propositions attributed to Jansenius) to 1794 (condemnation of the Italian Synod of Pistoia, near Florence).[16] Yet a mild form of Jansenism remained influential in Catholic piety, especially as regards reception of the Eucharist, well into the twentieth century.

To what extent these controversies—to which one may add the polemics between Bossuet (1627–1704) and Fénelon (1651–1715) over quietism and the possibility of *l'amour pur*[17]—affected the average understanding of grace and justification remains a moot point. The volume of Jean-Martin Moye (1730–1793) entitled *Le Dogme de la Grâce* (published in 1774 at Nancy, but written before 1769) may serve as a witness to the doctrine of grace of the period among well-informed authors who were not professional theologians.

The book is a synthesis of the Catholic doctrine of grace, destined to enlighten the laity on the holiness to which they are called. It is divided in four parts: I, the nature of grace; II, the operations and progress of grace; III, the obstacles to grace; IV, the means to obtain grace. Grace, an undeserved gift from God, is "above nature, does not come from nature, is not due to nature."[18] The author's point of view is radically dynamic: grace is not seen primarily as a created entity placed in the soul, but as an action of God's. It is something that God does so that we in turn may act "supernaturally." Moye is familiar with the distinction between habitual or sanctifying grace and actual grace, the terms which had come to replace the medieval expressions *gratia gratum faciens* and *gratia gratis data*. Yet a common purpose united them. "Although habitual grace alone can justify us and merit heaven for us, nevertheless all grace is oriented to justification and eternal salvation."[19]

The distinctions made during the quarrel *de auxiliis* are listed: grace is sufficient or efficacious, immediate or mediate. More basically, Moye distinguishes grace of the Creator and grace of the Redeemer, graces for one's own sanctification and graces for the sanctification of others, exterior graces and interior graces, graces of light and graces of strength.[20] Among the graces that are "the most necessary to salvation," Moye mentions the graces of vocation, of justification, and of predestination:

> The grace of vocation is that by which God calls us to faith; the grace of justification is that by which he forgives our mortal sins and, from sinners that we were, makes us just; it is the same as sanctifying or habitual grace, of which we have spoken. The grace of predestination is a preparation of the means by which all those who will be saved will be saved infallibly.[21]

Moye takes no side on the two main theologies of predestination (before or after God's foreknowledge of human merit). He insists rather that this is "an impenetrable mystery,"[22] that the number of the elect is very small, and that in any case "predestination, at least in its application, implies two things: graces and even very special, on God's part, and cooperation with grace on man's part." Without the first, man cannot be saved; without the second, "God will not save man."[23]

Sanctifying grace is the "grace of adoption," which gives us "the quality of children of God" and places in us the basis for merit: this is "the charity which reigns between God and us, insofar as we love him and we are loved by him."[24] It is identical with justifying grace, yet this expression adds a nuance of its own:

> To speak exactly, sanctifying grace is that by which our mortal sins are forgiven and we become pure and holy; for holiness means exemption from crime and purity of soul. Justifying grace signifies something more: profession of the theological and cardinal virtues which bring us to the fulfillment of all justice and the practice of good works.[25]

The category of merit poses no problem for Jean-Martin Moye, since merit results from grace, and by no means precedes or prepares it. "It is grace alone which, lifting man above himself and above nature, insufflates in him a wholly divine strength in order to act in a supernatural way which makes his actions agreeable to God and worthy of heaven."[26] Yet we do not now live in the mode of glory. Rather, "grace is distributed on earth, and glory is given in heaven." Still, grace is already totally admirable, in its principle, in its effects, and in its goal. It "has as its principle the three Persons of the Holy Trinity, which equally contribute to its communication to us." Its effect is "to make us participate in the divine nature."[27] Its goal is "to lead man to eternal life."

In this way Moye reduces to the unity of divine action the multiplicity of graces as he has enumerated them. The categories of theology and spirituality should not becloud the fundamental oneness of grace as God's action. This comes out well in the following passage:

> All these graces are formally distinguished, since each presents us with a different idea; yet they are taken one for the other; they are in fact, mutually and morally, the same grace, because they are always united and inseparable; one presupposes and enfolds another: as soon as God forgives our sins, he sanctifies us by pacifying our soul; he justifies us by giving us his grace, the gifts and the virtues which are inseparable from it; henceforth we cannot fail to please him, to be agreeable to him, being clothed and adorned with his gifts, with his charity: he loves us and gives us the grace to love him, he takes us as his children, he communicates his Spirit to us, he promises us his kingdom.[28]

Analysis of the unity of grace does not rest there. Jean-Martin Moye is acquainted with the distinction between created grace (graces) and Uncreated Grace. Chapter II of Part IV includes some admirable pages on the scriptural words for grace. One of them is "spirit":

> Finally, since it is the Holy Spirit who inspires and moves our spirit by his grace, so that grace in its principle is no other than the very Spirit of God working in us through his grace—what theologians call Uncreated Grace—although the gifts of this

> Grace which are communicated to us—and which theologians call
> created graces—are distinguished from the Holy Spirit as the
> effect from its cause, the Scripture often designates them with the
> one word, spirit. . . . [29]

There is no need for our purpose to record Moye's discussion of
the marks of predestination, which, as he carefully points out, do not
amount to the assurance of predestination which the Council of Trent
condemned as a "presumptuous temerity" of Calvinists.[30] Nor do we
need to analyze Moye's treatment of the effects of grace. In fact, the
last three parts of the book amount to a treatise on the spiritual life,
in which the negative aspect, the struggle against obstacles, is inserted
between two positive descriptions—of the divine action in the progress
of grace (Part II) and of human involvement in this progress through
prayer, trust in Jesus Christ, the communion of saints, and the sacraments (Part IV). One could find in this structure the traces of an
original approach to spirituality, but examination of this point would
take us away from our topic.

Clearly enough, the overall category is not justification. It is
grace. In this, Moye exemplifies well the dominant tendency of Catholic theology in modern times. Several of the categories which arrested
Luther's attention find their place. Justification is the movement by
which God takes us from injustice to justice, from impiety to piety,
from enmity to friendship. Faith is that to which we are basically
called. Trust focuses all attention on the Christological center of faith
and life. But Moye—and in this too he is typical of most Catholic
authors, then and since—is not directly acquainted with Luther's
analysis of justification and the ensuing problematic. The language of
imputation finds no echo in Moye. Yet there is something like *justus
et peccator* in the contention, which is at the heart of Part III, that
"we are always slaves of our vices and desires."[31] Above all, a traditional formula, which derived from medieval mystics and was familiar
to Luther, appears in good place: "One must place oneself in the hands
of God like soft wax, ready to receive such an imprint as will please
him."[32]

While Jean-Martin Moye was working out his theology of grace
in his missionary endeavors, the doctrine of justification which had

presided over the Reformation was exposed to its severest test by a man who, like Moye, did not claim to be a theologian, was an avid reader of the *Imitation of Christ,* was concerned about "simplicity of intention and purity of affection,"[33] was also a great missionary and an undaunted traveler, yet who reached widely divergent conclusions from those of the French priest. John Wesley (1703–1791) was, almost singlehanded, the architect of what has been called the "Wesleyan reaction in the evolution of Protestantism."[34] The story has been told, and the theological aspects of Wesley's thought analyzed, many times. It will suffice for our purpose to indicate the main points of Wesley's doctrine.

To speak of Wesley's doctrine is not to suggest that he claimed originality. He did not. He simply wanted to maintain and emphasize the doctrine on grace and justification which he read in the Thirty-Nine Articles and the Homilies[35] which were official in the Church of England, and which he considered to be faithful to the Scriptures. Yet only after a certain evolution in his life and thought did Wesley place this doctrine, as he understood it, at the center of his concerns and of his preaching. Raised in a High Church manse, son of a scholarly Anglican priest and a warmly devout and theologically cognizant mother, influenced by the Non-Jurors and later by the Moravians, John Wesley progressively discovered the Lutheran doctrine of justification by faith alone.[36] But the high point of this discovery was a vivid experience of its truth in his heart rather than an intellectual conviction of its correctness. This vivid experience, which was itself prepared in Wesley's own search and anxieties, was recorded in a famous passage of his *Journal,* for Wesley was a faithful journal-keeper. The date is Wednesday, May 24, 1738:

> . . . In the evening I went very unwillingly to a society in Aldersgate Street, where one was reading Luther's Preface to the Epistle to the Romans. About a quarter before nine, while he was describing the change which God works in the heart through faith in Christ, I felt my heart strangely warmed. I felt I did trust in Christ, Christ alone for salvation; and an assurance was given me that he had taken away *my* sins, even *mine,* and saved *me* from the law of sin and death. I began to pray with all my might for those who had in a more especial manner despitefully used me and

persecuted me. I then testified openly to all there what I now first felt in my heart. . . .[37]

Wesley himself relates this experience to the doctrine of justification, to renunciation to his "own righteousness," to the dialectic of Law and Gospel, to an explicit "continual prayer for this very thing—justifying, saving faith, a full reliance on the blood of Christ shed for *me,* a trust in him, as *my* Christ, as *my* sole justification, sanctification and redemption."[38] The kinship of such language to that of Luther is patent.

It is of course well known that Wesley had been influenced early by Moravian pietism, which itself derived from Lutheranism. His mother Susanna had deep admiration for the Moravians,[39] of whom she made the acquaintance through her reading when John was only eight years old. Her favorite son felt at home in their warm piety, especially after crossing the Atlantic with a group of Moravians in 1733. Yet it was not through their agency that he was initiated to the doctrine of justification by faith. This he had already found in the *Homilies.* In fact, the authors of the *Homilies,* and Archbishop Cranmer, their editor and possibly their chief author, were under the doctrinal influence of Calvin rather than of Luther.[40] Wesley's grasp of the teaching of the *Homilies* emerges from some of his sermons, in which he professes to abbreviate them, thus providing his audience with the quintessence of their doctrine:

[And the true sense] of this doctrine—*we are justified freely by faith without works* . . . —is not that this our own act, to believe in Christ, or that this our faith in Christ, which is within us, doth justify us (for that were to account ourselves to be justified by some act or virtue that is within ourselves), but that although we have faith, hope and charity within us and do never so many works thereunto, yet we must renounce the merit of all, of faith, hope and charity and all other virtues and good works which we either have done, shall do, or can do, as far too weak to deserve our justification.[41]

There is thus a virtue called faith, and good works do merit something. Yet neither suffices for justification. One should therefore, in Wesley's words, "trust only in God's mercy and the sacrifice which Christ offered for us on the Cross." Thus it already appears that, whereas Wesley always maintained the doctrine of justification by faith, this was no longer Luther's doctrine. Among the Moravians, Wesley met also with an altered doctrine of justification by faith, since Zinzendorf added to Luther's sober description and interpretation a large dose of the enthusiasm originally condemned in the *Schwärmer.* Admittedly, Wesley extolled at first Luther's doctrine on justification. A few days after the Aldersgate experience, in a sermon at St Mary's, the university church of Oxford, he proclaimed:

> "By grace you are saved through faith" ... It is this doctrine, which our church justly calls *the rock and foundation of the Christian religion,* that first drove Popery out of these kingdoms; and it is this alone that can keep it out.[42]

Yet one may indeed wonder if Wesley's understanding, at that moment, was identical with Luther's. When Wesley, soon afterward, travelled to Germany, visited Herrnhut and met with Zinzendorf, he was so pleased with what he found that he even compared the count with "his divine Master."[43] On his return to England, he wrote to the Herrnhut community in most un-Lutheran terms: "We are endeavoring here also, by the grace which is given us, to be followers of you, as ye are of Christ."[44] To become a follower of any man, be he the holiest, is of course entirely foreign to the Christocentric structure of Luther's faith.

The pietism of the Moravians was to remain with Wesley even after he grew cool toward them, which happened as early as 1740–41. Wesley found himself repelled by the quietism of some Moravians and the ensuing disaffection from the sacraments and institutional means of grace ("outward ordinances").[45] From the beginning of his preaching career, Wesley proclaimed the necessity of good works. His early tract on *The Character of a Methodist* hardly mentions faith, but stresses love, joy, purity of heart: "All the commandments of God he accordingly keeps, and that with all his might. For his obedience is in proportion to His love."[46]

This was far from Luther's ethos. Wesley's violent reaction is therefore not surprising when, for the first time, he read Luther's

Commentary on Galatians. His comment, as recorded in his Journal for June 15, 1741, is colorful and significant:

> I was utterly ashamed. How have I esteemed this book, only because I heard it so commended by others; or, at best, because I had read some excellent sentences occasionally quoted from it! But what shall I say ... ? Why, not only that the author makes nothing out, clears up not one considerable difficulty; that he is quite shallow in his remarks on many passages, and muddy and confused almost on all; that he is deeply tinctured with mysticism throughout, and hence often dangerously wrong. ... How does he decry reason, right or wrong ... as an irreconcilable enemy to the gospel of Christ! ... Again, how blasphemously does he speak of good works and of the law of God! ... But who are thou that "speakest evil of the law and judgest the law"?[47]

On the evening of this disappointed conclusion, Wesley preached, and he noted the day after: "After reading Luther's miserable comment upon the text (Gal 6:15), I thought it my bounden duty to warn the congregation against that dangerous treatise, and to retract whatever recommendation I might ignorantly have given of it."

Wesley's reaction is not only emotional. He very carefully draws the line between himself and Luther. While he still professes to teach justification by faith, this is not Luther's conception. Wesley distinguished between justification and sanctification. In the words of the first Annual Conference of the Methodist Societies (June 1744), justification means "to be pardoned and received into God's favor and into such a state that, if we continue therein, we shall be finally saved."[48] It is a gift; but its previous condition is faith, defined as "a spiritual sight of God and the things of God." And faith itself has a previous condition:

> But must not repentance and works meet for repentance go before Faith? Without doubt, if by repentance you mean conviction of sin, and by works meet for repentance, obeying God as far as we can, forgiving our brother, leaving off from evil, doing good and using his ordinances according to the power we have received.[49]

Wesley may affirm, in a sermon, that "a man is justified by faith without the deeds of the law, without previous obedience to the moral law, which indeed he could not, till now, perform."[50] He may say that the only condition for it is faith. Yet he also provides a series of tests to discover if one "be in the faith." One of these runs as follows:

> He (i.e., the man in the faith) no longer judges it (i.e., holiness) to be an outward thing, to consider it either in not doing harm, in doing good, or in using the ordinances of God. He sees it is the life of God in the soul; the image of God fresh stamped on the heart; an entire renewal of the mind in every temper and thought, after the likeness of Him that created it.[51]

Thus Wesley restored a *facere quod in se est* as a condition for faith and thereby for justification.

> Both repentance and fruits meet for repentance are, in some sense, necessary for justification. But they are not necessary in the *same sense* with faith, nor in the *same degree*. Not in the *same degree,* for those fruits are only necessary *conditionally* if there be time and opportunity for them. . . . Not in the *same sense,* for repentance and its fruits are only *remotely* necessary—necessary in order to faith—whereas faith is *immediately* and *directly* necessary to justification. It remains that faith is the only condition which is *immediately* and *proximately* necessary to justification.[52]

Remotely necessary or not, the requirement of repentance and fruits for faith, which is itself required for justification, nullifies Luther's *simul justus et peccator.* Moreover, Wesley introduces degrees in justification itself. The last entry in his Journal for the year 1739 contains the following passage:

> . . . I believe,
> 1. There are degrees in faith, and that a man may have some degree of it before all things in him are become new; before he has the full assurance of faith, the abiding witness of the Spirit, or the clear perception that Christ dwelleth in him.
> 2. Accordingly, I believe there is a degree of justifying faith (and

consequently, a state of justification) short of, and commonly antecedent to this.[53]

Actually, Wesley's chief interest does not really lie in justification, but in sanctification, "which is indeed in some degree the immediate fruit of justification, but nevertheless is a distinct gift from God and of a totally different nature."[54] The foundation for this distinction is Trinitarian: "The one implies what God *does for* us through his Son; the other, what he *works in* us by his Spirit." As the Son and the Spirit work together, although differently, Wesley can say: "And at the same time that we are justified—yea, in that very moment—*sanctification* begins."[55] Sanctification inspires "the character of a Methodist." It leads directly to the heart of Wesley's concerns—Christian perfection.

This expression, which is borrowed from William Law's volume bearing that title, embodies Wesley's conviction that total holiness is possible in the present life, and that on the basis of the New Testament one can "fix this conclusion: a Christian is so far perfect as not to commit sin."[56] For the first Annual Conference, to be sanctified is "to be renewed in the image of God, in righteousness and true holiness."[57] Faith is its condition and instrument. The growth of faith marks increase in sanctification. Wesley likes to see sanctification arising from a special moment, a unique experience, an event in the soul which he calls "the New Birth." This is more important than justification, for, in his words, "Justification implies only a relative, the new birth a real change."[58] Justification only removes guilt; new birth takes away "the power of sin." The first is outward; the second, inward: "a vast inward change, a change wrought in the soul, by the operation of the Holy Ghost, a change in the whole manner of our existence. . . . " If justification and new birth may happen to coincide in time, yet they are vastly different, "of wholly distinct natures." Wesley waxes eloquent when he describes this new birth and the inward testimony of the Holy Spirit which is inseparable from it.

New birth is only a moment, but it starts the process of growth to perfection. It is "the gate" of sanctification. "Then our sanctification, our inward and outward holiness begins; and thenceforward we are gradually to 'grow up in Him who is our Head.'" On the analogy of human growth, Wesley adds: "The same relation which there is between our natural birth and our growth, there is also between our new birth and our sanctification."[59]

Wesley writes in his *Plain Account:*

> ... to this day both my brother and I maintained (1) that Chris-
> tian perfection is that love of God and our neighbor which implies
> deliverance from *all sin;* (2) that this is received merely *by faith;*
> (3) that it is given *instantaneously,* in one moment; (4) that we
> are to expect it, not at death, but *every moment;* that now is the
> accepted time, *now* is the day of this salvation.[60]

How can one experience now and at every moment something which
is given instantaneously in one moment? Wesley has created a
dilemma, which could have been the occasion for reflection on the
structure of time in Christian experience. But Wesley's genius is not
speculative. The dilemma is resolved practically, not intellectually. It
disappears when the Gospel is formulated in terms of Law: there is a
Law of Christ to be obeyed and practiced at every moment. Through
obedience to the new Law, every moment re-enacts the original instantaneous experience of new birth. If the instantaneous moment may be
called Gospel, the constant obedience of every moment is to Law. But
these are one. Methodist preachers are advised to preach "Law and
Gospel mixed together."[61] To forget the dimension of Law brings
directly to Moravian quietism.

Such a stress on Law, on obedience, on doing what is in us in
regard to growing in perfection entails a reliance on the human self,
enlightened and transformed by grace, which was entirely foreign to
the reformers. Wesley becomes acutely aware of this when some of his
adversaries dub on him the qualificative "Arminian." Arminius
(1560–1609) had, against Calvin, asserted the power of the human
will to cooperate with divine grace, thus restoring a synergism which
the reformers had denied. Perfection, then, seems to have a double
source, God and oneself. Wesley rejected the two-source idea, for perfection is the work of the Holy Spirit in our will, yet he accepted the
label, placing it in the very title of the periodical which he started in
1778, *The Arminian Magazine.* While his reaction to Luther was
chiefly marked by rejection of Moravian quietism, denunciation of the
Commentary on Galatians, and restoration of the Gospel as Law of
Christ, Arminianism was the mark of Wesley's opposition to the Calvinist orientation of some early Methodists, like the preacher George
Whitefield (1714–1770) and the wealthy protectress of Methodism,

the Countess of Huntingdon (1707–1791). But by the same token, Luther's emphasis on the unfree will and on harlot reason was equally rejected. In other words, nothing was left, in Wesley's mature writing, of Luther's justification by faith. This may be illustrated with some questions and answers from *Farther Thoughts on Christian Perfection:*

> *Q.*—How, then, are we "not without law to God, but under the law of Christ" (1 Cor 9:21)?
>
> *A.*—We are without that law; but it does not follow that we are without any law; for God has established another law in its place, even the law of faith: and we are all under this law to God and to Christ: both our Creator and our Redeemer require us to observe it.
>
> *Q.*—Is love the fulfilling of this law?
>
> *A.*—Unquestionably it is. The whole law under which we now are is fulfilled in love (Rom 13:8–10). Faith working or animated by love is all that God now requires of man. He has substituted (not sincerity but) love, in the room of angelic perfection.[62]

Wesley finally praises in love the long-suffering quality that Luther found intolerable: "It suffers all the weaknesses of the children of God, all the wickedness of the children of the world. . . . "[63]

That Wesley's views on the human part in justification and holiness had considerable influence on later Protestant thought need not be argued here. That they marked a recovery of older Catholic truths or a convergence with the Catholic theology of his time may also be defended with persuasive arguments. But it will be more in keeping with the scope of the present inquiry to try to assess the situation at the beginning of the nineteenth century as regards the doctrine of justification. The Wesleyan movement has broken the unanimity of Protestantism. The Counter-Reformation has lost most of its momentum under the blows of the French Revolution. The doctrinal picture has become more variegated than ever.

A sophisticated attempt to put the colors of the theological spectrum in a logical order was made by John Henry Newman, who will provide us with the conclusion of this chapter. Newman's *Lectures on Justification,* published in 1838, comprise thirteen lectures and a long technical appendix. Newman was Anglican at the time. But his "advertisement to the third edition," written in 1874, asserted: "Unless the author held in substance in 1874 what he published in 1838, he would not at this time be reprinting what he wrote as an Anglican."[64]

The heart of the problem, for the initiator of the Oxford Movement, lies in determining "the formal cause" of justification. Newman finds four main positions:

> (1) It has been said that we are justified directly and solely upon our holiness and works wrought in us *through* Christ's merits *by* the Spirit; or (2) upon our holiness and works *under* the covenant of Christ's merits, or, in other words, sanctified and completed by Christ's merits; or (3) that our faith is mercifully appointed as the substitute for perfect holiness, and thus is the interposing and acceptable principle between us and God; or (4) that Christ's merits and righteousness are imputed as ours, and become the immediate cause of our justification, superseding everything else in the eyes of the Judge. Of these the first is the high-Roman view; the last the high-Protestant; and the two intermediate are different forms of what is commonly considered the high-Church view among ourselves, and very nearly resemble Bucer's among Protestants, and that of Pighius, Mussus and many others of the Roman school.[65]

Newman acknowledges that there exist other positions: among Protestants, "some say that faith is the formal cause, some forgiveness of sins, some the imputation of Christ's righteousness, and some that there is no formal cause at all."[66] The Protestants that Newman has in mind in this volume are chiefly Anglican Evangelicals. But their doctrines are carefully compared with the views of Luther, especially in the *Commentary on Galatians* of 1535, as also with the doctrines of Melanchthon, Bucer, Calvin, Richard Hooker, Gerhard, and a number of lesser authors. We already know that Luther's commentary of 1535 is more polemical than that of 1519. The formulas are more paradoxical, the tone more vehement. Luther constantly attacks the doctrines and practices of the *phanatici*. Yet Newman, ignoring this polemical context, takes Luther's extreme formulas literally, at face-value. This is clearly a flaw in his reading of Luther's great commentary. As to Catholicism, Newman explains that "indeed it is no point of faith among them . . . to take the view which I have called Roman, but still I shall so call it . . . as being the generally received, orthodox, and legitimate exposition of their formularies."[67] His picture of Catholic doctrine derives from the Council of Trent and the *Roman Catechism,* compared both to Scholasticism and to the Counter-Reformation. The description of Anglican thought draws chiefly on the *Homilies.*

Newman's thesis is both simple and subtle. He locates a broad consensus between high-Romanism and high-Protestantism. For high-Romanism, justification is an inherent righteousness manifested through works which are the works of the Spirit in us. For high-Protestantism it is an awareness by faith of Christ's merits being imputed to us regardless of our performing the works of faith, a conception which Newman illustrates with "the paradox of Luther . . . *fides justificat sine et ante charitatem,* faith justifies without and before charity."[68] The consensus of the *via media* holds that "justification comes *through* the sacraments, is received *by* faith, *consists* in God's presence, and *lives* in obedience."[69] This corresponds to the two middle views mentioned above. It is, according to Newman, not only the standard Anglican doctrine, but also that of the Strasbourg Reformer Bucer and of many Roman Catholics. It is even reflected, if not explicitly taught, in many passages of Melanchthon and of Luther himself. It is also the main doctrine of the Church Fathers. This central position is analyzed at length in the bulk of the *Lectures,* where it is related to sacramental theology, liturgy, Christology, and the experience of holiness. It justifies the irenic judgment of the older Newman, in his "advertisement to the third edition," that the drift of the *Lectures* is "to show that there is little difference but what is verbal in the various views on justification, found whether among Catholic and Protestant divines."[70]

V.

LUTHER IN CATHOLIC THOUGHT

That Luther's doctrine of justification was misunderstood by his opponents in the polemics of the sixteenth century can be illustrated with abundance. And no doubt the fault lay partly with Luther's fondness for paradoxical expressions and polemical exaggerations. But his occasional stretching of language to its limits cannot excuse the frequent practice of his adversaries of ascribing to him the opposite of what he meant. Luther could not recognize his doctrine in this affirmation of so balanced a person as St. Thomas More: " . . . he orders that they should only believe that they will be saved only by faith in Christ, and even that they should neglect not only ceremonies but even all kinds of good works."[1] This may stand for us as a relatively moderate sample of a misrepresentation of Luther's doctrine which has at times bordered on the ludicrous and the scurrilous.

Recent Catholics have themselves inherited this polemical anti-Luther tradition. Before paying special attention to the doctrine of justification, modern Luther studies by Catholics have therefore had to face the previous question: How should Luther as man and as theologian be understood? The basic problem has been to overcome the tradition initiated by Johannes Cochlaeus, who, although he was a respectable theologian, had shown himself to be an extremely biased historian. Catholics who were primarily influenced by Cochlaeus' history could not take Luther's theology seriously because they would not respect the man. Yet even though the Cochlaeus tradition was widely accepted through the Counter-Reformation, the pre-Tridentine desire to arrive at an irenic consensus on the matter of justification did not die with the failure of the *Regensburg Book* to be accepted by either side, and with the adoption of a decree on justification at the sixth session of the Council of Trent. The eighteenth century theologian Ildefonz Schwartz (1752–1794) was still—and already—able to write:

It is noteworthy that even the main point about which the Reformation was concerned, the doctrine of justification, is now explained on both sides in an all but completely different way, and that the distance in this one doctrine is not so great as it seems.[2]

As a point of comparison with this irenic judgment, one may look at what Matthias Scheeben (1835–1888) wrote about the doctrine of the reformer. Scheeben summed up this doctrine as a belief in a purely forensic justification effected "only on the basis of faith."[3] This, as he explained, implies the "imputation of the righteousness of Christ" by a merely juridical decision of God, which is indeed gratuitous but remains unrelated to the actual state of the person; the human will is uninvolved, "entirely passive," in the process of justification. This is far from what Luther said in his commentaries on Galatians.

By the time of the First Vatican Council, the context of the problem had changed. The three centuries between Trent and Vatican I had seen tremendous changes in the Church. Whereas the two sides in the sixteenth century were intensely religious, the Vatican Council had to formulate the faith in opposition to its negation. Rationalism, scientism, and positivism challenged not one interpretation of faith, but faith itself. The assumption was that a modern man cannot believe; faith would be a denial of reason.

The Council was not the first Catholic reaction against rationalism. In the course of the nineteenth century, traditionalism had explained the achievements of human reason by a revelation at the origin of humankind. The Council had to distinguish between the tradition and traditionalism in looking at the relation between faith and reason.

The structure of the constitution *De Fide Catholica* (April 1870) is simple. After two chapters on God as Creator (chapter 1) and Revealer (chapter 2), which explain the origin of faith in the revelation, a chapter studies the nature of faith in its "supernatural" aspect (chapter 3). A final chapter investigates the relation between reason and faith and the legitimate activities of reason outside the realm of faith (chapter 4). Thus both rationalism and traditionalism are avoided.

One may distinguish between faith as God's act and faith as our own act. As God's act, faith has three aspects. There is, first, revelation as the presentation by God himself of what to believe. This took place at a certain moment in time through the incarnation (chapter 2). There is also an assistance of God through external helps which are like arguments in favor of revelation (chapter 3). There is finally an internal assistance extended by God to the believer. The Council calls it an "attracting and helping grace," an "internal assistance of the Holy Spirit," an "illumination and inspiration of the Holy Spirit," a "gift from God," an "efficacious support from a higher power," explained as an attraction to faith and a preservation in faith.[4] Thus, faith is God's act, not only in that it is known through revelation and supported by signs or miracles, but also in that we are attracted to it by God himself and assisted by him in believing and throughout the life of faith.

As to our own act, it is described as "full obedience of our will and intelligence." In this act "we believe that what he has revealed is true," we assent to the preaching of the Gospel, and we freely obey his grace.[5]

The relation between our act and God's act is called an assent and a cooperation.[6] But the mode of this cooperation is not explained, presumably because the Council did not wish to take sides in discussions on free will and grace. It is only suggested that, as the internal and external aspects of God's intervention work as one act, so also the act of God and our own activity work together as one.[7] In faith there is therefore some sort of experience which makes us one with God. And the Council specifies that "without faith . . . justification never happens to anyone. . . ."[8]

The relation between faith and reason is the more complex as it gives rise to several distinct problems, of which I will mention two.

First, there may be a natural knowledge of the formulations of faith before one comes to believe, or a philosophical acceptance of the existence of God before knowing him through faith. This is dealt with in chapters 3 and 4, in connection with the reasonable character of faith. The argument of the Council is that, to make faith reasonable,

God has joined to the inner light of faith some external signs of revelation, facts of experience which show God's power and knowledge at
work. "Right reason proves the foundations of faith."[9] Thus the problem changes. The question which has now to be solved bears on the
exact scope of this possibility of demonstration. In other words, what
is the meaning of "foundations"? Are these foundations of faith anterior to or constitutive of faith? Are we certain of revelation before
believing, or do we have to wait for faith itself to have the certainty
of revelation? But in this case, what would be the true value of the
signs of faith?

One may surmise that the Council took its clue from a previous
encyclical of Pius IX (*Qui pluribus,* November 9, 1846),[10] where the
foundations of faith had been identified as the elements which point
out its truth, that is, its divine origin. The conciliar text reduces the
longer list of the encyclical to two main kinds of facts, "miracles and
prophecies." It explains that such signs are adapted to everybody
because they show the omnipotence and infinity of God, two attributes
which anyone can at least roughly grasp. Consequently, it would seem
that for the Council the reasonable character of faith is inherent in
faith itself. Before the act of faith, there may be a knowledge of doctrinal formulas but there can be no conviction of their truth.

Second, since in the act of faith God does not take the place of
the human mind and soul, the believer's mind does accomplish the
operations proper to its psychological structure. What, then, is the
function of reason in the formation of the act of faith? This is precisely
the crux of all attempts to analyze faith. As was to be expected, the
Council does not side with any particular theology. Its view of the
structure of faith remains sufficiently general to cover several theological explanations:

> Faith is a supernatural power *(virtus),* by which, the grace of God
> attracting and supporting us, we believe that the things which
> have been revealed by him are true, not because of their intrinsic
> truth being perceived by the natural light of reason, but on
> account of the authority of the revealing God himself, who can
> neither be misled nor mislead.[11]

In other words, reason in the act of faith perceives that God's
authority is engaged in the revelation. But the First Vatican Council

makes no suggestion as to how this perception is obtained. On such a question one can find many ideas in the numerous studies of Christian or Catholic apologetics which followed the rejection of Modernism by Pius X. The period between the two world wars saw many such investigations.[12] But the answers proposed to the questions left pendant by Vatican I do not seem to me of great import in solving the more basic problem of the nature of justification.

One could of course wish—but it is too late to remedy the matter—that Vatican I, after considering faith as knowledge related to human reason, had studied it as the fundamental experience of God, the basis for all further spiritual experience. For if it is true that faith is "the foundation and root of justification," it implies much more than a certain compatibility with human reason. Justification implies an indwelling of the Three Persons in the one who is justified. Faith is an experience, however obscure, of the coming of the divine Trinity. Had Vatican I taken the problem of faith where Trent had left it, it would have narrowed the gap between the Lutheran and the Catholic traditions. It would by the same token have removed one of the difficulties which were at the root of the Modernist crisis. Instead, its concern for reason could but widen the gap.

The absolute necessity of grace for faith had been stressed at the Council of Orange. At Trent, Catholic thought had seen faith as a meeting point of the divine and the human, in the metaphysical, logical, and psychological order, and as the foundation and root of justification. At Vatican I reason was held to have a positive function in relation to faith. But this did not say anything about self-awareness as the constitutive element of personality, of the self as spirit. Faith cannot be only an acceptance of teachings proposed from the outside. It is, too, the reception of an interior light, by which one is gratuitously raised to the highest exercise of personality, the perception that God calls us just when we know ourselves to be sinful.

Among the factors which make possible a new assessment of Luther's doctrine, pride of place belongs to the renewal of Luther studies among Catholics. This was initiated by Johannes Lortz's two volumes on the Reformation in Germany. Lortz emphasized, among other things, Luther's debt to Nominalism, which Lortz considered to have been largely Pelagian.[13] He therefore popularized the notion that

Luther's earlier Catholicism was not fully Catholic.[14] Thus, Luther's later reaction against Pelagianism and Nominalism would have initially been a healthy search for the authentic Catholic tradition. Yet it would have been distorted, through later polemics, in an excessively one-sided subjective direction.

It is difficult today to endorse all of Lortz's positions and assumptions. Yet there is no doubt that his pioneer work opened the way to the breakthrough of 1957, when Hans Küng published his volume on justification.[15] While Küng dealt with Karl Barth and not with Luther, he identified Barth's thought as the purest systematization of Protestant theology today, thus implying that his own conclusion could apply to the teaching of the reformers. This conclusion was simple and, in a way, radical: there is "complete consensus" between Barth's doctrine of justification and that of the Council of Trent.

Yet Küng betrays a certain ambiguity about his understanding of the Reformation doctrine. For he stresses that Barth departs from the reformers at some key points, and chiefly on the question of how interior is the transformation of the Christian by grace. "It must first be formally stated that Karl Barth clearly teaches the *interior justifying of man*. Not that he has denied the forensic justification of the reformers, but that he has revised and deepened it, taking it seriously in its divine character."[16] Referring to this intrinsic-forensic problem, Küng also asserts: "Our question regarding the *simul justus et peccator* cannot under any circumstances be the Reformation question. It cannot challenge the authenticity of divine justification."[17] In his conclusion, Küng quotes a number of recent authors to support the statement that "Barth does not stand alone . . . the greater number of leading contemporary Protestant theologians have given up the purely extrinsic declaration of justice."[18] Thus Küng indirectly tells us how he understands Luther's doctrine: Luther taught a purely forensic justification without any kind of interior transformation by grace. Yet Küng is not sure that this is historically quite correct: "It might be a good idea if there should be an exacting historical investigation by Catholics as well, into what extent the reformers did after all take a stand for purely forensic justification. What is going on in this area is frequently based on notions about the opponent which are entirely too stereotyped."[19] It seems to me—but Küng does not draw this conclusion—that the problem is rather to uncover the intent of the forensic justification formulas which Luther did use: Were these meant to exclude interior transformation by grace, or rather to emphasize that such transformation comes to us from God and Christ as from a source external to our being and ultimately independent of our actions? If the reformers' primary concern was to safeguard the gratuity of justification and the sovereignty of God in the act of justifying sinners, then the Reformation doctrine does not "challenge the authenticity of divine justification." And if the chief concern of the Council of Trent was to protect the reality of the interior transformation wrought by grace in the sinner, then the two theologies may tend to speak different languages, but without necessarily excluding each other's intention.

The reaction to Küng's thesis was generally favorable among Catholic authors, but less so among Lutherans, who seem to have been taken by surprise. Their problem was not with Küng's assessment of Protestant teaching, though differences between Barth and Luther were more marked than appeared in his book. It had more to do with skepticism as to the accuracy of Küng's description of Catholic doctrine: Could the wide divergences of past polemics have really dwindled to so little? Time was obviously required for Lutheran authors to take cognizance of the broad consensus of recent Catholic thought and piety: both had slowly veered away from concern about the merits of virtues and good actions to a more fundamental emphasis on the gratuitousness of justification and sanctification. In Catholic theology at least, the possibility of agreement with Luther was no longer a utopia.[20]

Otto Pesch, who has devoted a lengthy volume to Luther's doctrine on justification compared to that of St. Thomas, sums up the situation of the last decades in the following way. From a generally negative judgment on Luther as man and as theologian, Catholic scholars passed to "an understanding of Luther which . . . *excuses* the tragic results of his reforming thoughts and actions, without yielding to him in any essential point." From there the situation rapidly evolved toward a more positive appreciation: "Now Catholic theology is being introduced to a Luther whom it, in spite of criticism on individual points, seriously tries to understand as a *real possibility for its own theological thought and life, without* beforehand trying to devaluate any of the decisive elements which go together to make the theologian, preacher and reformer, Martin Luther." Yet I wonder if this description of the present state of things is not over-optimistic. The extensive researches into the theology of redemption made, among others, by Jean Rivière (1878–1946) and Louis Richard (1880–1956) did not open any gate in the direction of Luther's view of justification. The studies of sacrifice which were instrumental in the growth of the liturgical movement between the two world wars—e.g., by Emile Masure—ignored the questions raised by Luther and the Reformation.

I have found no openness to Luther's doctrine of justification in Henri Rondet's *Gratia Christi,* a book which was widely acclaimed when it appeared in 1948.[22] One can honestly ask who among contemporary Catholic theologians and authors has recognized Luther's theology of grace as an acceptable option. Does such an option remain a matter of special historical research? Is it an advanced ecumenical outreach? Does it find a place in the study of grace in the average Catholic seminary?

Already in 1954, Louis Bouyer, in his largely autobiographical volume, *Du Protestantisme à l'Eglise,*[23] began to rehabilitate Luther's concept of justification in Catholic eyes, though this did not go without a sharp critique of some points in the reformer's doctrine. Bouyer made a clear distinction between two aspects of Luther's theology.

On the one hand, the reformer's intentions were perfectly traditional and orthodox. Luther wished, against the Pelagian tendencies of the nominalists and the humanists, to re-emphasize the gratuitousness of salvation on God's part, the sovereign lordship of Christ in the task of redemption, the recognition of this gratuitousness and the awareness of this lordship in faith, the total disproportion between what a human person can do or deserve and the always unmerited gifts of forgiveness and new life from God. Thus it is by grace alone that we are saved, and through faith alone that we are notified of salvation. This, as Bouyer showed, has nurtured Protestant piety through the centuries. It is in harmony with what the Council of Trent taught in the decree of its sixth session. Bouyer quoted with deep appreciation a page of Luther's *Commentary on Galatians,* 1535 (chapters 3, 13), commenting: "All this passage shows better than any laborious explanation what renewal of apostolic Christianity and of its traditional interpretation, in keeping with the Fathers of the Church, the Lutheran insight would have been, and has been, and remains in fact for the best of Protestantism. . . . "[24]

On the other hand, Bouyer believed that Luther's basic insight had been rendered relatively ineffective by "the negative elements of the Reformation." As regards justification, these took the form of a theory of forensic justification, with which Luther was led, through the polemics in which he was involved, to identify the doctrine of *sola gratia*. Likewise, Luther was led to oppose *sola fide,* not only to the works of the old law and to the apparently good works performed by man as sinner before the reception of divine grace, but also to the good works of man as made just by the power of Christ. Luther's attacks on the Scholastic concept of "faith informed by love" were particularly disastrous, as this concept had originally no other purpose than to embody the concern that faith must be a living faith—Luther's very concern.

It was partly under Bouyer's influence that in 1958 I wrote the following page, which however went somewhat further toward a positive understanding of Luther's overall doctrine:

> If we take the words literally, a purely extrinsic justification cannot make us just in anybody's eyes. The *fiat* which saves us must be a creative *fiat:* it causes what it enunciates, and it makes us just in complete reality. Is this denied by the reformers? It would appear not. When they asserted imputed justification, they wished simply to deny a justice pertaining to man; they wished to make Pelagian distortions of sanctification impossible, to kill at the roots the "idolatrous" desire to sanctify oneself through an accumulation of merits. In other words, imputed justification has a very profound sense if we truly understand the thought of the reformers; the inmost being of the Christian is no longer the sinful creature that it was before Christ, but a being-in-Christ, and it is in Christ's own Person that we receive forgiveness, salvation and grace, sanctification and glory. We have nothing of our own: all comes from Christ. As men we are sinners, but as Christians we are saved. Thus, as the Lutheran saying puts it, the Christian is "always sinful, always penitent, always justified"; sinful in himself, his justification is Christ: "God acquits us of guilt by extending to us the justice which pertains to the Lord Jesus." There is

no doubt that this is the sense of the term "imputation." Calvin makes it explicit: "From this it follows clearly that we are justified in the sight of God by means of the justice of Christ alone; that is, man is not just in himself but only through the justice of Christ which he receives through imputation." So "imputed" justice is given to man in a real way. The ambiguity of the term "imputation" is regrettable, but once this has been cleared up, the doctrine is not heterodox.[25]

Karl Rahner's judgment has generally been favorable to Hans Küng's thesis: "The fact remains, as we think, that Küng's book has achieved an astonishing result: the consent of a great Protestant theologian to a presentation of a doctrine of justification which must be considered as capable of and needing improvement on certain points, but which cannot be designated as un-Catholic. One can be a Catholic and hold this doctrine of justification, which Barth has declared to be his own."[26] This judgment does seem slightly condescending and triumphalistic: Barth is to be judged by Catholicism, while Catholicism does not seem to be in need of being judged by Barth. Rahner, however, returned to the problem from a different angle in an essay on *simul justus et peccator,* in which he investigated the formula of the reformers themselves.

The idea that the Christian is *simul justus et peccator* represents, for Rahner, the heart of the Reformation doctrine of justification. The notion that this is "something merely extrinsic, 'forensic,' a pure 'as if' " is only a "subsequent theological interpretation, which can only obscure the original starting point of the formula."[27] What this formula basically means is that man "cannot be saved of himself and by his own power. Grace, justification and salvation arise from God's mercy alone. Man is always and everywhere dependent on this justifying mercy of God. This is the correct starting point for the Protestant formula: *simul justus et peccator.*"[28]

To this description of the state of justified man, Catholics must, in Rahner's judgment, answer both a *no* and a *yes.*

Catholic theology rejects the formula "just and sinner at the same time" because it does not render the state of man in an objectively correct and adequate manner. The ultimate, basic formula of human existence is not a suspended dialectic between sinfulness and holiness. Man has really crossed the boundary of death. In the ultimate view, in view of God's action which has become effective in him, man is no longer sinful and justified at the same time, but justified and nothing else.

I understand this to mean that the formula is wrong if its purpose is to describe God's action, for God's action does indeed make a sinner *justified.* Yet one must also say "yes" to *simul justus et peccator,* because it is a *sinner* who is then justified.

Yet Rahner locates a Catholic "yes" at three levels. First, Catholic teaching leaves the faithful uncertain of the extent to which divine grace has in fact withdrawn them from their original basic sinfulness:

If justification has really taken place, then this man is no longer a sinner but the justified and sanctified man. . . . Can the individual, however, maintain with absolute certainty about himself that *he* is really someone justified and that, precisely because he is this, he is no longer a sinner? According to the teaching of the Council of Trent there is no absolute individual certitude about salvation.[30]

Second, in regard to "the permanent sinfulness of man by venial sins," Rahner sees Catholic teaching as being very close to Luther's view of the sinner: "We are in fact sinners who hope always to be allowed to escape again out of their sinfulness into the mercy of God."[31]

Third, the state of pilgrimage in which we are in this life makes it impossible to regard total justice as being already ours, for even when we are justified by grace, we carry within us the sinfulness from which we come:

We come from Adam and the land of darkness and look for the eternal light and bright perfection. Since the one great movement of our existence out of our lost condition towards God always still carries within itself the source from which this movement originates, we are "just and sinners at the same time" by being sinners in the state of becoming who are still in search of perfection.[32]

Rahner concludes that *simul justus et peccator* is acceptable to Catholic theology, "if only the factors of a Catholic *no* to this formula remain clear."[33] Whether, as thus qualified by Rahner, the formula still adequately expresses the Reformation insight into the nature of justification is of course the moot question. Should it, as accepted by Rahner, no longer correspond to what Luther intended to mean by it, then we may have a verbal but by no means a real agreement.

It seems quite impossible to guess what proportion of Catholic theologians today would agree with Rahner's analysis of *simul justus et peccator* and with the implied harmony between the Catholic understanding of justification and at least one major aspect of Luther's doctrine. Those who have judged other points of Luther's theology favorably would presumably accept Luther's doctrine of justification insofar as it is of a piece with the doctrines they have studied at greater length.[34] Yet, as indicated above, I suspect that the mass of Catholic theology professors in seminaries, universities and colleges have not seriously looked at Luther's theological insights. It also seems to me that Rahner's irenic assessment does not go far enough. The question is not whether Catholics can admit Luther's doctrine on justification in a sense which is not quite that of Luther himself. It is whether they can truly recognize the evangelical and therefore Catholic intent which underlies Luther's more or less adequate formulas. If they can do so, then the theology of Luther is not simply a theology with which they ought to dialogue. Rather it emerges as a valid alternative to their own traditional formulations of the Christian Gospel.

Vatican Council II did not address these questions directly. It did not discuss the nature of justification. Yet it did provide a brief description of faith in its constitution *Dei Verbum,* on divine revelation. It is significant that, within a few lines, the Council quotes St. Paul, Vatican I, and the Council of Orange.

To God who reveals himself is due the "obedience of faith," by which man freely pledges himself to God, giving "God the full submission of his intelligence and will" and voluntarily assenting to the revelation he has made. For such a faith to be born, man needs to be prepared and assisted by God's grace and the interior helps of the Holy Spirit, who will move and turn the heart to God, open the eyes of the mind, and give "all men joy in consenting to and believing the truth." Unceasingly, the same Holy Spirit so perfects faith through his gifts that the understanding of revelation may become more profound (n. 5).[35]

The conciliar stress on "understanding" should not soften the emphasis on "full submission" and on faith as "obedience." The allusion to a preparation of faith, to "free pledge" and to "voluntary" assent should not be read as excluding the basic belief that this is entirely the work of grace in the believer. As I wrote in 1966, in a commentary on the constitution *Dei Verbum,* "The faith with which we answer this coming down of God toward us is much more than intellectual assent. . . . In order to be full, this assent of the will and the intellect must proceed from the whole human personality and include, besides consent to what is said, trust in Christ, commitment, hope and love."[36] The text of Vatican II attempts to overcome the over-intellectual conceptions of faith which have been frequent in Catholic theology since the Counter-Reformation. By the same token, it should help to bring Catholics and Lutherans closer together in their understanding of faith and justification.

That Martin Luther was a religious genius can readily be admitted even by those who cannot accept all his conclusions or who regret the harsh tone of his polemics. That he should be considered a doctor of the universal Church is a more controversial proposition, yet one that should be seriously considered.

In his central doctrine of justification by faith, Luther was right, and the conditions of his times made him a strenuous defender of the truth. This strikes me as the inescapable conclusion from an unbiased reading of his less polemical writings. To be right on a peripheral question would of course not justify making anyone a doctor of the Church. But the irony of Luther's situation is that he was right on the chief point of the Christian understanding of human life in its relationship to God, at a time when the Church's hierarchy, caught in the exciting turmoil of the Renaissance and the power politics of the emerging European nations, was blind to the point he was making.

Luther's centrality to the history of the Christian doctrine of grace in the West has been brought out in the preceding pages. The core of his reflection—the doctrine of justification—belongs to the whole Christian world. The analogy of his teaching with those of Augustine and the Council of Orange among the Fathers, and, in

Scholasticism, with the positions of Thomas Aquinas, should give Luther pride of place in Catholic studies of the theology of grace. Even his forensic language need no longer be offensive. In fact, it may well be necessary. Thus, one can read the following lines in a rather conservative investigation of grace by an author who is by no means inclined to Protestantism:

> The theme of his book is the threefold pattern of the impact of grace in our lives: first, as habitual grace . . . secondly, as actual grace . . . thirdly, and more problematically, it is experienced in God's particular interventions in our conscious lives, as it were from the outside.[37]

Here the adverb "problematically" hardly tones down the forensic aspect of the experience of grace, "as it were from the outside." Likewise, a great Catholic mystic of our century, Adrienne von Speyr, emphasized the forensic nature of grace in the following text:

> Grace is what comes exclusively from God, to what we can never assimilate ourselves, what we can but receive and never becomes our own property, what we may communicate but never becomes our own substance. Grace therefore remains always in God, and even when we transmit it, it is God who transmits it, in spite of us.[38]

If we remember that Luther himself had been under the influence of at least one branch of Catholic mystical thought and experience, this quotation may suggest that there is an experiential affinity between his theology of grace and the conviction of many Catholic mystics that, in the words of one of them, "it is God who does everything."[39] Had Luther's language been compared in his time with that of the mystical tradition, the judgment of the Catholic hierarchy could have been very different from what it was. To the mystics too, man is "nothing" before God; human actions, even at their finest, are "like dung" before the power and the holiness of divine grace; reward is not given to merit. Rather, all comes from the divine initiative, from God's gratuitous love to those who remain unworthy of it. The proper locus for discussion of Luther's insight into faith and grace is not the theology of Scholasticism, but the experience of the presence of God. The companion figure of Luther, for comparison and contrast, should not be Thomas Aquinas but John of the Cross.

Even without entering deeply into the frame of mind of the classical mystics of Catholic Christianity, it seems clear that Luther stands near to them in the conviction that it is in the breakdown of all human support systems that one is the most likely to grasp the liberating and reconciling power of divine grace. At that very point where one is totally abandoned, and not before, can faith in the one Incarnate Lord who is the only Mediator and Savior seize and transform us. Not to periods of human self-satisfaction or triumphant ecclesiasticism does Luther's theology speak, but to periods of despair, darkness, and insecurity—such as our own period.

Admittedly, an objection will not fail to come to the mind of modern readers: Is not Luther's forensic language, in his description of justification, germane to what Maurice Blondel called "extrinsicism" or Paul Tillich called "heteronomy,"[40] and which both these authors rightly rejected? Extrinsicism was unacceptable to Blondel because it would make a true relationship to God impossible. Heteronomy was condemned by Tillich because it would contradict the theonomous dimension of existence and life. Forensicism in Luther is precisely that which safeguards the divine character of grace and makes real the transformation of the sinner. Precisely on this point, past misunderstandings may be illustrated with the following remark made by Ludwig Wittgenstein: "In logic the most difficult standpoint is that of sound common sense. For in order to justify its view it demands the whole truth; it will not help by the slightest concession of construction."[41] If we substitute "justification" for "sound common sense," we obtain a good rule of thumb to assess the value of a doctrine of justification: by its very nature it must imply the entirety of the Christian Gospel; it demands the whole truth. Polemics on justification have always arisen from partial or piecemeal perceptions of Christian truth.

Yet there is more. As Luther speaks of justification, this is not for him a doctrine among others; not simply a piece in the edifice of Christian belief, although it is also that; not only one ingredient in the analogy of faith. Luther uses justification as a test of doctrines, attitudes, commandments, and prohibitions; he makes it the touchstone of the Christian style of living and mode of thinking. In other words, he places justification by faith at the heart of theological methodology.

It belongs within the structure of theological method. It can be compared to a metalanguage in linguistics. That is, justification by faith should be treated not as the mark of a theological system or school, which could be related to and compared with others, but as the basic standard underlying all proper theological methods by which all theologies ought to be judged. Admittedly, other ways of affirming the centrality of the divine initiative may be proposed; other biblical or traditional categories may fulfill a like function. Indeed, no one can foresee what problems or conflicts of later times may require emphasis on other criteria of Christian thought and life. Even so, Luther's formulation of justification may well remain the most central and the most universal principle by which to test all other possible criteria of theology and theological method; it may be the principle of principles, the method of methods. This at least is the perspective in which the question of justification by faith should be envisaged if the divisions of the Reformation are to be ecumenically overcome.

Dialogues have been taking place since 1965 between Lutherans and Catholics concerning the divisive aspects of their doctrines. These dialogues have been focused on the Eucharist, the ministry, and authority in the Church,[42] rather than on justification. But the keystone to reconciliation between Luther and Catholic doctrines has to be their agreement on justification. The general feeling, which prompted the selection of topics to be discussed, was that justification had outgrown being a point of fundamental disagreement. I believe that this feeling is correct if justification is viewed as a doctrine among others, as a piece in the analogy of faith. Even here, however, the changes of problematic in regard to salvation, justification, and sanctification which have taken place in theology and life between the sixteenth and the late twentieth centuries still need to be officially acknowledged. Luther's doctrine on justification by faith needs to be recognized and endorsed as an expression of the perennial Catholic tradition.

But if justification by faith is not only a doctrine, but is also a central key to all Christian doctrine and life, then the entire edifice of Catholic thought since the sixteenth century stands in need of reconstruction. Properly understood in the sense which Luther recognized it, justification by faith is the core of the Gospel. One cannot be satisfied with simply accepting it, even affirming it. Once accepted and affirmed, it necessarily becomes the touchstone of all subsequent affirmations and proclamations. In its light the Church must reform itself. Sacramental theology and practice, liturgical worship, ethical principles and their applications, and the structure and nature of ministerial authority must be reviewed, reassessed and, where necessary, reconstructed. This may well be done in the spirit of Vatican Council II, which declared: "The magisterium is not above God's Word; it rather serves the Word. . . ."[43] The human actions of believers are not above faith, and should not be besides faith: their proper place is under faith. In other words, we are presented, in justification by faith, with what I have called elsewhere the critical principle of theology. And the theology in question is not that of individual authors; it is that of the *Ecclesia*. Theologians may properly choose their own foci and criteria in view of the context in which they work, and in pursuit of the intellection of faith that will be germane to the predominant concerns of their time and place. Meanwhile, the *Ecclesia* needs to steer its course protected from subjectivities, idiosyncrasies, eventually fads, which theologians are prone to promote. If the transcendent principle of this journey be the Holy Spirit, and the effective immediate principle of Christian life be divine grace, the doctrinal-linguistic formulation of these principles is justification by faith. One need not fear that traditional doctrines will be weakened thereby, or the biblical witness distorted. For the critical principle of theology is, as I have also shown, the key to its constructive principle. Doctrines will be preserved, but in the reconstructed form of a renovated theology.

It would therefore seem that the reformation initiated at Vatican II should now be pursued in the light of Luther's understanding of justification by faith. The day should come when Martin Luther must be rehabilitated by the *Ecclesia Romana* which he intended to serve but which, to his deep regret, he was led to identify, for his time, as the kingdom of antichrist. Then should we be able to rejoice in the good news that, at a critical moment when the understanding of God's justice was threatened by the accretions of late medieval piety and practice, Martin Luther was enabled to stand up for what was and remains the core of the Christian faith.

CONCLUSION

Martin Luther's posthumous destiny has not been unlike that of St. Augustine. The theologian of justification has followed the theologian of grace. Despite the abundance of their writings—or perhaps because of it—both have been widely misunderstood. The distortion of Luther's central thought started as early as Melanchthon's irenic attempts to reach agreements with Catholics on the one side and Calvinists on the other. It was even inscribed in the very structures of institutional Lutheranism when the Formula of Concord canonized the third use of the Law. As recently as 1963, the Lutheran World Federation, meeting at Helsinki, found itself unable to speak with one voice on the matter of justification and even to agree on the exact nature and scope of this *articulus stantis vel cadentis Ecclesiae.*[1] Nonetheless, in 1973 the report on "The Gospel and the Church," adopted at Malta by the joint Lutheran-Roman Catholic Study Commission, noted: "Today a far-reaching consensus is developing in the interpretation of justification"; yet when it went on to state that "justification can be understood as expressing the totality of the event of salvation,"[2] the Commission made the concept so broad as to encompass many theologies. In 1980 the Lutheran-Episcopal Dialogue in the USA was able to affirm more clearly "that we are accounted righteous before God only for the merit of our Lord and Savior Jesus Christ, by faith, and not for our own works or deservings."[3] Yet if one looks at the general picture of the Church since the Reformation, whether from a Catholic or from a Lutheran perspective, it does seem that the doctrine of justification by grace through faith, and not by merits of our own, has had little impact.

If indeed Luther was correct in identifying the article of justification as the stone at which the Church stands or falls, then the

Church, in its representatives, has chiefly stumbled on it. This is perhaps not surprising, if Enrico Di Negri is right in his judgment that Luther's doctrine on justification opened the sense of "becoming" which characterizes modern culture. The present life

> is not a being but a becoming; not a rest but the exercise of activity; nothing is already finished and consummated, but everything moves and advances.[4]

This sense of the ongoing march of created reality instores a Heraclitean *panta rhei* (everything keeps flowing) at the heart of the life of faith. Di Negri sees it encapsulated in Luther's striking formula: *de non esse per fieri ad esse* (from non-being, through becoming, to being). But it is a characteristic of institutions, and above all of religious institutions, that they acquire and convey a false security by entertaining a mistaken sense of being, of remaining stable like an island in a stormy ocean. Lutheranism, as an institution, has paid lipservice to justification by faith, but it has also vied with other institutions and established itself in security. It was against such a search for security in the past for the sake of the present that Vatican Council II reacted when it tried, with mixed success, to renounce triumphalism.

Meanwhile, however, the sense of fluency, of becoming, of always moving onward, has passed to the secular world and its philosophies. Utopias of progress, of Marxist promises or dreams, of future liberation have embodied it in our times. And by a curious irony, it now is, from these tainted sources, re-entering the churches in the dubious forms of process philosophy, of eschatological evangelism, of praxis theology, of several political and liberation theologies.

Yet this climate of the present moment may be an opportunity. The time may have come, in the contemporary ecumenical dialogue among the still divided Christians, for making a new effort to understand the meaning of Luther's doctrine of justification by faith and its right place at the heart of Christian life and thought. This doctrine, by its very nature, withdraws us from both the cult of institutions and the cult of actions. Away from these, there must be divine grace, for nothing is then left on which one can rely. In the words of the future Paul VI, this greatly misunderstood prophet of our time,

The sensible world by itself does not point to the things of the kingdom of God: and this is why we are incapable to accept the message of faith. This is too spiritual. But if, with my modern myopic eyes, with my modern avid eyes, I could interpret the material alphabet of the immaterial spirit, joy would return, and trust. The trust, that grace is near and is easy. Coming nearer, making easier. That the atmosphere which I breathe and which invades me is filled with the Holy Spirit. . . . [5]

And, lest one fear that such a trust should lead to self-righteousness, Montini adds:

I will not see all: the mirror remains, the enigma remains. . . .

NOTES

Chapter I

1. Rather than provide an extensive bibliography at this point, I refer the reader to John Reumann's study of justification in the New Testament, written for discussion in "Lutherans and Catholics in Dialogue," which is the official dialogue between the two churches in the USA. For other recent literature, see Benno Przybylski: *Righteousness in Matthew and This World of Thought,* New York, 1981.

2. I have culled this idea from my friend Alejandro Diez Macho, in his book, *Indisolubilidad del Matrimono y Divorcio en la Biblia,* Madrid, 1968, p. 18; but I am not sure all philologists would agree.

3. On the structural method in general, see Claude Lévi-Strauss: *Structural Anthropology,* Garden City, N.Y., 1963, pp. 202–231; A. J. Greimas: *Du Sens. Essais sémiotiques.* Paris, 1970, pp. 117–230. On structural method and theology, see my volume, *La Théologie parmi les sciences humaines,* Paris, 1975. On the use of the method in exegesis, see Daniel Patte: *What Is Structural Exegesis?* Philadelphia, 1976; Edgar V. McKnight: *Meaning in Texts. The Historical Shaping of a Narrative Hermeneutics,* Philadelphia, 1978.

4. The "faith of Jesus" is a central category in some recent Christologies, e.g., Jan Sobrino: *Christology at the Crossroads,* New York, 1976, pp. 79–145; James P. Mackey: *Jesus, the Man and the Myth,* New York, 1979, pp. 159–171. Sobrino writes: "The term 'Jesus' faith' . . . seeks to sum up the whole thrust of Christology in recent years . . . " (p. 81). This is undoubtedly an exaggeration, but it does illustrate the prejudices inherent in a Christology from below. See my remarks in *Images of the Christ,* Washington, 1981, ch. V, note 11.

5. For a somewhat different light on Saul's "conversion," see Krister Stendahl: *Saul among Jews and Gentiles,* Philadelphia, 1976, pp. 7–23.

6. The relevance of this expression may be seen in that "the way" will be a major ethic-religious category in early Christian literature.

7. The religious symbolism of "the city" has been explored by John S. Dunne: *The City of the Gods. A Study in Myth and Morality*, New York, 1965, pp. 81–161.

8. "Myth" should not be taken in a derogatory sense. A myth is a complex of symbols; and symbols assist thought in transcending empirical conditions to perceive their eternal ground and meaning. See *La Théologie parmi les sciences humaines*, pp. 82–93. The suggestive ideas in Claude Lévi-Strauss: *Myth and Meaning*, Toronto, 1978, need to be completed by an investigation of the religious discussion of myth.

9. On the importance of vision as the visual equivalent of myth, see my *The Vision of the Trinity*, Washington, 1980; William Purdy: *Seeing and Believing. Theology and Art*, London, 1976.

10. On the centrality of the "in Christ" category in Pauline doctrine, see Lucien Cerfaux: *Christ in the Theology of St. Paul*, New York, 1959; Rudolf Bultmann: *Theology of the New Testament*, Vol. I, New York, 1955, pp. 175–180. For a more modern approach see Ernst Käsemann: *Perspective on Paul*, Philadelphia, 1971; *Commentary on Romans*, Grand Rapids, 1980.

11. Recent scholarship is divided on the extent of Luke's acquaintance with the doctrines of Paul. See Bultmann, 1. c., Vol. 2, pp. 116–118; H. Conzelmann: *The Theology of St. Luke*, London, 1960; E. Franklin: *Christ the Lord. A Study in the Purpose and Theology of Luke-Acts*, Philadelphia, 1975. If Luke is indeed the author or the redactor of the pastoral Epistles, he must have known Paulinism, which he modified in restating it, such a modification being presumably intentional; see Stephen G. Wilson: *Luke and the Pastoral Epistles*, London, 1979.

Chapter II

1. Origen's text survives in Rufinus' Latin translation, P.G., 17, 539–632; John Chrysostom's homilies are in P.G., 60, 583–682. One may wonder what inspired the original impulse to see the Scriptures as writings to be commented upon, rather than simply to be read or to be believed. Was the primary purpose purely homiletic and exhortatory? Or was the notion of theological deepening of and penetration into the text already operative? While the second motive would seem better to correspond to Origen's method, the first would fit John Chrysostom's circumstances. Yet one may presume that there were earlier attempts at commentary, of which we can now know nothing.

2. Marius Victorinus, on Gal., Phil., Eph., in P.L., 8, 1145–1294; Ambrosiaster on most of the Pauline corpus, in P.L., 17, 47–536; Pelagius' commentary is in Alexander Souter: *Pelagius's Exposition on the Thirteen*

Epistles of St. Paul, 3 vols., Texts and Studies, Vol. 9, nn. 1–3, Cambridge, 1931.

3. Augustine's anti-Pelagian works are many, from *De natura et gratia,* 413–415 (P.L., 44, 247–290) to his unfinished last work, *Contra secundam Juliani responsionem imperfectum opus,* 429–430 (P.L. 45, 1049–1608). Earlier, Augustine had taken free will for granted: *De diversis questionibus ad Simplicianum* q.2, 22 (P.L., 40, 127–128).

4. See Gustave Bardy: *La Conversion au christianisme durant les premières siècles,* Paris, 1949.

5. *De Trinitate,* I, 2 (P.L., 10, 27). Because Hilary spent four years of exile in Phrygia, 356–360, he is a major witness to the unity of Greek and Latin thought in his time, despite the growing separation between Greek and Latin language areas and cultures; see C.F.A. Borchardt: *Hilary of Poitiers' Role in the Arian Struggle,* Bois-le-Duc, Netherlands, 1966.

6. P.L., 10, 28.

7. *Ibid.,* 32.

8. *Ibid.,* 33.

9. *Ibid.,* 36.

10. Psalm 118, nun, 20 (CSEL, 22, p. 412) and ain, 10 (*ibid.,* p. 501). See Charles Dhont: *Le Problème de la préparation à la grâce. Débuts de l'Ecole franciscaine,* Paris, 1946, pp. 31–34.

11. See Jaroslav Pelikan: *The Emergence of the Catholic Tradition, 100–600,* Chicago, 1971, pp. 278–331.

12. Faith gives *perfectam cognoscentiam* (perfect knowledge) of God, in Marius Victorinus: *Ad Candidum,* 32, 6–10 (S. Chr., 68, Paris, 1960, p. 172).

13. *Ibid.,* pp. 9–89.

14. On the life and times of Augustine, see Peter Brown: *Augustine of Hippo,* Berkeley, 1967; on his conception of grace, see J. Patout Burns: *The Development of Augustine's Doctrine of Operative Grace,* Paris, 1980.

15. *Retractationes,* I, 23, 2 (B.A., XII, Paris, 1950, p. 414). Where convenient, I indicate the date of Augustine's writings, according to the chronology included in Franciscus Moriones: *Enchiridion Theologicum Sancti Augustini,* Madrid, 1961, pp. 706–721.

16. See Georges de Plinval: *Pélage, ses écrits, sa vie et sa réforme,* Lausanne, 1943.

17. *De praedestinatione sanctorum,* 4, 8 (P.L., 44, 965–966).

18. *Contra Julianum libri sex* (423) IV, 4 (P.L., 44, 756).

19. *De moribus ecclesiae catholicae* (387–389) I, 22, 40 (P.L., 32, 1328).

20. *Contra Julianum* . . . IV, 104 (1401).

21. *Tractatus in Johannis evangelium* (413–418) XIV, 13 (B.A., 71, Paris, 1969, p. 752). For recent surveys of the doctrine of original sin, see Edward Yarnold: *The Theology of Original Sin,* Cork, 1971; Henri Rondet: *Original Sin. The Patristic and Theological Background,* New York, 1972.

22. *De correptione et gratia,* II, 4 (P.L., 44, 918).

23. *De gratia Christi et peccato originali* (418) (P.L., 44, 370).

24. D.S., nn. 222–223; 226–230.

25. *De gratia Dei et libero arbitrio,* II, 10 (P.L., 58, 832).

26. D.S., n. 375; canons 6 and 7 are in nn. 376–377.

27. D.S., nn. 398–399.

28. Jean Devisse: *Hincmar, archévêque de Reims, 845–882,* Geneva, 1975, Vol. III, p. 1412, note 1.

29. Dhont, *op. cit.,* p. 278, note 80.

30. Henri Bouillard: *Conversion et grâce chez saint Thomas d'Aquin. Etude historique,* Paris, 1944, pp. 111–114.

31. Dhont, *op. cit.,* p. 278.

32. Devisse, *op. cit.,* Vol. III, p. 1411; on these canonical collections, see Paul Fournier-Gabriel Le Bras: *Histoire des collections canoniques en occident,* 2 vols., Paris, 1931–1932; Gonzalo Martinez Diez: *La Coleccion Canonica Hispana,* Madrid, 1966. Text of *Dionysio-Hadriana* in P.L., 67, of *Hispana* in P.L. 84.

33. Dhont, *op. cit.,* p. 278.

34. Southern Gaul had precisely been the chief battleground over semi-Pelagianism. Presumably, the tradition of the Council of Orange was still alive there. In fact the southerners were more Augustinian than the northerners in the predestinarian controversy.

35. *Sententiae,* II, 6 (P.L., 83, 606).

36. I summarize here too briefly the story told at length by Devisse, *op. cit.,* I, pp. 187–279. On Gottschalk, see C. Lambot: *Oeuvres théologiques et grammaticales de Godescalc d'Orbais,* Louvain, 1945; Jean Jolivet: *Godescalc d'Orbais et la Trinite. La méthode de la théologie à l'époque carolingienne,* Paris, 1958.

37. Text among the works of Hincmar, P.L., 125, 63–64.

38. Devisse, *op. cit.,* I, p. 137–138.

39. His *Liber de praedestinatione* is in P.L., 122, 355–440; see Cyrille Cappuyns: *Jean Scot Erigène,* Louvain, 1933. Besides Gottschalk, Hincmar and John Scot, the main participants in the controversy were Rabban Naurus, who started it by condemning Gottschalk (*De praedestinatione,* P.L., 112, 1530–1553), and who supported Hincmar; Ratramnus (*De praedestinatione Dei,* P.L., 121, 12–80) and Florus of Lyon (*Sermo de praedestina-*

tione, P.L., 119, 95–102; *Liber adversus Joannem Scotum*, 101–250), who opposed Hincmar. Prudence of Troyes (*Epistola ad Hincmarum et Pardulum*, P.L., 115, 971–1010; *De praedestinatione contra Joannem Scotum*, 1009–1352) adopted a mediating position, yet more Augustinian than that of Hincmar. The doctrine of John Scot was more Greek than those of the two main parties.

40. Texts of the Council of Valence in D.S., nn. 625–633.

41. Text among the works of Hincmar, P.L., 126, 123. The expression rendered as "to give what is just" is *reddere meritum*. One may perceive here the semantic richness of the Latin term *meritum*. Meaning, fundamentally, "justice as deserved," it can be taken in the sense of "reward," and of the basic quality or worth which gives title to a reward, but also in the sense of "gift or benefaction," which is itself undeserved and in turn deserves gratitude. (See L. Quicherat: *Thesaurus Poeticus Linguae Latinae*, 2nd. ed., Paris, 1875, p. 672.) Thus, between God and man, meritum may be located in man as deserving a reward from God; but it may also be understood as a benefaction received from God without previous merit. The latter sense is still close to the surface of the language of the Synod of Douzy. It will practically disappear in the Scholastic discussions of *meritum de congruo* and *de condigno*.

42. P.L., 126, 123–124.

43. P.L., 126, 125.

44. *Cur Deus homo* I, 11 (S. Chr. n. 91, Paris, 1974, p. 264). St. Thomas will carefully distinguish beween two human justices, a purely natural one, which is founded on the human reason and establishes the structures of civil society, and a *justitia fidei*, which has its principle in *prophetia*, that is, revelation, and which provides the strength of that *societas hominum secundum quod ordinatur ad finem vitae aeternae*, that is, of the Church (*De veritate* q. 13, a. 3, ad 2). See Walter Ullmann: *A History of Political Thought in the Middle Ages*, Baltimore, 1965; *Law and Politics in the Middle Ages*, Ithaca, N.Y., 1975.

45. *Op. cit.*, II, 16, p. 410.

46. *Ibid.*, I, 12, p. 268.

47. *Ibid.*, I, 9, p. 250.

48. *Ibid.*, I, 20, p. 320.

49. *Ibid.*, II, 10, p. 384.

50. See Nikolaus Paulus: *Geschichte des Ablasses im Mittelalter*, 3 vols., Paderborn, 1922; for a modern theological reflection, see Karl Rahner: *Remarks on the Theology of Indulgences (Theological Investigations*, Vol. 2, 1963, pp. 175–202). Studies of the sacrament of penance usually provide some information on the question of indulgences, which is historically related

to the development of penance, e.g., Bernard Poschmann: *Penance and the Anointing of the Sick,* New York, 1964, pp. 210–232.

51. *De concordia* . . . P.L., 158, 494.

52. *Ibid.,* 496.

53. *Ibid.,* 494.

54. *Ibid.,* 506.

55. *Ibid.,* 516.

56. *Ibid.,* 534–535.

57. *Ibid.,* 521–522.

58. *Ibid.,* 523–524.

59. *Ibid.,* 526.

60. *Ibid.,* 527.

61. *Ibid.,* 530.

62. *Ibid.,* 531–532.

63. *Ibid.,* 537.

64. D.S., nn. 728, 739. Abelard was in open reaction against his former teachers, Anselm of Laon (d. 1117), whom he despised, calling him "smoke without flame," and William of Champeaux (c. 1070–1121), who was Anselm of Laon's disciple. Anselm of Laon had himself studied under Anselm of Canterbury. Yet Abelard professed admiration for the latter; see Jean de Ghellinck: *L'Essor de la littérature latine au XIIe siècle,* Vol. I, Bruxelles-Paris, 1946, p. 48.

65. D.S., n. 725.

66. See the standard studies of medieval exegesis: Ceslaus Spicq: *Esquisse d'une histoire de l'éxégèse latine au moyen âge,* Paris, 1944; Beryl Smalley: *The Study of the Bible in the Middle Ages,* 2nd ed., Oxford, 1952; Henri de Lubac: *L'Exégèse médiévale,* 4 vols., Paris, 1959–1964; G.W.F. Lampe, ed.: *The Cambridge History of the Bible,* Vol. 2, Cambridge, 1969.

67. Quoted in Dhont, *op. cit.,* p. 75.

68. *Summa Alexandri,* pars III, inq. I, tr. I, q. V, me. III, corpus and ad 6 (Quaracchi, vol. IV, 1948, pp. 993–995).

69. Odo's works have remained unprinted; see Dhont, *op. cit.,* pp. 161–185.

70. *Commentary on the Sentences* II, d. 25, p. 1, q. 3. I quote from the standard edition, in *Opera Omnia,* Quaracchi, Vols. 1–4, 1882–1902.

71. *Ibid.,* d. 24, p. 1, a. 1, q. 2, ad 2.

72. *Ibid.,* d. 26, q. 1.

73. *Ibid.,* d. 26, q. 2.

74. *Ibid.,* d. 27, a. 1, q. 1.

75. *Ibid.,* d. 27, a. 1, q. 2.

76. *Ibid.,* d. 27, a. 2, q. 2.
77. *Ibid.* d. 27, a. 2, q. 3.
78. *Breviloquium,* part V, ch. 2, n. 3. For an English translation of this work, see José de Vinck: *The Works of Bonaventure,* Vol. II, Paterson, N.J., 1960.
79. *Ibid.,* n. 4.
80. *Ibid.,* n. 5.
81. *Ibid.,* C.S., II, d. 28, a. 1, q. 2–3.
82. *Ibid.,* a. 1, q. 1.
83. *Ibid.,* a. 2, q. 1; see *Brev.,* V, ch. 2, n. 3.
84. *Ibid.,* d. 28, a. 2, q. 3.
85. *Ibid.,* III, d. 33, q. 4.
86. *Ibid.,* d. 20, q. 1–6.
87. *Ibid.,* d. 33, q. 2, ad 4.
88. *Ibid.,* d. 19, a. 1, q. 1.
89. *Ibid.,* d. 23–32. In Bonaventure's language, the "faculties" can be "reduced" to the substance of the soul. Reduction is in fact a favored process in Bonaventurian thought. It consists basically in envisaging a product or result from the standpoint of that which it comes from or in which it inheres. The method adopted in the *Breviloquium* attempts to reduce everything to its highest principle. The word "reduction" is not well rendered by "full analysis," as in Ewert Cousins' translation of the *Itinerarium* (*The Soul's Journey into God,* New York, 1978, p. 82), for reduction is synthetic, not analytic. See Tavard: *Transiency and Permanence. The Nature of Theology according to St. Bonaventure,* St. Bonaventure, N.Y., 1954, pp. 104–105.
90. C.S., IV, d. 17, q. 1, a. 2, sol. 1.
91. *Ibid.,* I, d. 17, q. 1, a. 3.
92. *Ibid.,* II, d. 27, q. 1, a. 4, ad 4.
93. S.T., III, q. 112, a. 2, q. 1, ad 1 and ad 3.
94. *Ibid.,* q. 112, a. 2.
95. *Ibid.,* q. 109, a. 6.
96. *Ibid.,* q. 114, a. 6.
97. *Ibid.,* q. 114, a. 6, ad 1.
98. *Ibid.,* q. 113, a. 3.
99. *Ibid.,* q. 113, a. 4.
100. *Ibid.,* I, q. 23, a. 2.
101. *Ibid.,* q. 23, a. 3.
102. See Wolfhart Pannenberg: *Die Prädestinationslehre des Duns Skotus,* Göttingen, 1954.

103. *Opus oxoniense,* II, d. 25, q. un., n. 22, in *J.D. Scoti Opera Omnia,* Paris (Vives) 1891–1895, Vol. 13, p. 221 b.

104. *Reportata parisiensia,* II, d. 7, q. 3, n. 13 (l. c., vol. 22, pp. 630 b-631 a); the version of this important text in the manuscript F 69 of Worcester Cathedral is slightly different: Dhont, 1. c., p. 288, note 16. On grace as an accident, see Thomas Aquinas, S.T., III, q. 110, a. 2, ad 2–3.

105. See Dhont, *op. cit.,* p. 292, note 27.

106. *Op. cit.,* II, q. 7, a. 3, n. 13 (Vol. 22, p. 630 b).

107. *Opus oxoniense,* IV, d. 14, q. 2, n. 13 (Vol. 18, p. 70 b).

108. In the eyes of Scotus, Aquinas makes God an *acceptor personarum* (Vol. 22, p. 630 b); on predestination, see *Opus oxoniense,* I, d. 41, q. 1, n. 11.

109. See Heiko Oberman: *Archbishop Thomas Bradwardine, a Fourteenth-Century Augustinian. A Study of His Theology in Its Historical Context,* Utrecht, 1957; on the problem of justification in late Scholasticism, see Paul Vignaux: *Justification et prédestination au XIVe siècle: Duns Scot, Pierre d'Auriole, Guillaume d'Occam, Grégoire de Rimini,* Paris, 1934.

110. Heiko Oberman: *The Harvest of Medieval Theology. Gabriel Biel and Late Medieval Nominalism,* Cambridge, Mass., 1963, p. 123.

111. A.E. McGrath: *The Anti-Pelagian Structure of 'Nominalist' Doctrines of Justification* (*Ephemerides Theologicae Lovanienses,* April 1981, ann. lvii, fasc. 1, pp. 107–119).

112. I follow here McGrath, *op. cit.;* in this case, however, one should ask who were the Pelagians denounced by staunch Augustinians of the later Middle Ages, such as Thomas Bradwardine (c. 1295–1349), author of *De causa Dei contra Pelagium et de virtute causarum ad suos Mertonenses libri tres,* and Gregory of Rimini (c. 1280–1358) in his *Commentary on the Sentences.* Thomas Bradwardine opposed both the Averroists as determinists and the Ockhamists and Nominalists as Neo-Pelagians. But was he correct in this? It would seem that misunderstanding of Nominalist theology started early. Furthermore, many of the Renaissance humanists opted for a form of Pelagianism, which they attributed to Jerome, seen as an opponent of Augustine; see Heiko Oberman: *Archbishop Bradwardine,* pp. 11–15, 29–48, 206–211; *Werder und Wertung der Reformation,* Tübingen, 1977, pp. 82–105.

Chapter III

1. Quoted in Clyde L. Manschreck: *Melanchthon, the Quiet Reformer,* New York, 1958, p. 129. Melanchthon was taken by surprise at Luther's marriage, of which he had not been informed and to which he had not been invited, presumably because he was expected not to approve of it.

2. Hans J. Hillerbrand: *Landgrave Philip of Hesse,* St. Louis, 1967; see the account of the affair in Manschreck, *op. cit.,* pp. 261–276.

3. See *Doctrinal Agreement and Christian Unity. Methodological Considerations (ARC-DOC. Documents on Anglican-Roman Catholic Relations,* Vol. I, Washington, 1973, pp. 49–53); this is a joint statement issued by the Anglican-Roman Catholic Commission in the USA.

4. Johannes Cochlaeus (1479–1552), a canon of Worms Cathedral, was the author of *Commentaria de actis et scriptis Martini Lutheri,* 1549, a book which had considerable influence in distorting the image of Luther in the mind of most Catholics for several centuries. As a theologian, however, Cochlaeus, who polemicized with most of the major reformers, is quite respectable; see my volume, *Holy Writ or Holy Church. The Crisis of the Protestant Reformation,* New York, 1959, pp. 124–129.

5. Reference will be made to the Weimar edition (W.A.) of Luther's works: *Luthers Werke,* especially Vol. 2, 1884 and Vol. 40, 1914. This reference, Gal. 5, 12, W.A., Vol. 2, p. 513. After checking the standard English translation of the two commentaries on Galatians (*Luther's Works,* Vol. 26–27, St. Louis, 1963–1964), I found it too inaccurate to be followed. Another translation of the commentary of 1535—which itself results from a revision of the first English version, published in 1575—may be consulted, Philip S. Watson, ed.: *A Commentary on St. Paul's Epistle to the Galatians,* Westwood, N.J., 1953. The bibliography of Luther's doctrine on justification is of course abundant; see the titles mentioned in *Jose Martin-Palma: Gnadenlhere von der Reformation bis zum Gegenwart,* Freiburg, 1980.

6. W.A., vol. 2, pp. 446–447.

7. *Ibid.,* p. 447.

8. *Ibid.,* p. 448.

9. Ch. 1, 4, p. 458.

10. Ch. 1, 10, p. 464.

11. John Dillenberger, ed.: *Martin Luther. Selections from His Writings,* New York, 1961, p. 53.

12. Ch. 1, 11, p. 466.

13. Ch. 1, 6, p. 460.

14. Ch. 1, 6, p. 461.

15. Ch. 1, 11, p. 466.

16. Daniel Olivier: *La Foi de Luther,* Paris, 1978.

17. Ch. 2, 17, p. 495.

18. Ch. 2, 18, p. 497.

19. Ch. 2, 19, p. 498.

20. Ch. 2, 18, pp. 496–497.

21. Ch. 2, 19, p. 500. Luther stresses the difference between signifier

and signified; contemporary structural analysis tends to stress their unity; see Ferdinand de Saussure: *Cours de linguistique générale,* Paris, 1971, pp. 97–103.

22. Ch. 2, 19, p. 499.

23. *The Ascent of Mount Carmel,* bk. II, ch. 28–31, in Kieran Kavanaugh and Otilio Rodriguez: *The Collected Works of St. John of the Cross,* Washington, 1973, pp. 202–211.

24. Ch. 2, 16, p. 489.

25. Ch. 2, 16, p. 490.

26. Dillenberger, *op. cit.,* p. 88.

27. Ch. 2, 21, p. 504.

28. Ch. 2, 21, p. 503.

29. Ch. 4, 8, p. 538.

30. Ch. 5, 1, p. 560.

31. *La Théologie parmi les sciences humaines,* Paris, 1975, pp. 63–64.

32. *The Mythical Structure of the Church,* in *Journal of Ecumenical Studies,* Vol. 9, n. 2, Spring 1972, pp. 352–355.

33. Ch. 3, 27, p. 529.

34. Ch. 3, 29, p. 531.

35. Ch. 4, 4–5, pp. 535–536.

36. Ch. 5, 17, p. 586.

37. Ch. 2, 17, p. 495.

38. Ch. 5, 19, p. 589.

39. Ch. 5, 18, p. 587.

40. Ch. 3, 28, p. 530. For the spiritual tradition of kenosis or self-abandonment, Luther could draw on the *Theologia germanica.* An anonymous work related to Rhineland mysticism, this was composed in German, in or near Frankfurt around 1350. Luther published a shorter version of it in 1516 and a longer one in 1518, to which he gave the title by which it is now known. Self-abandonment is described, among other places, in chapter 33 (Bengt Hoffmann, ed.: *The Theologia Germanica of Martin Luther,* New York, 1980, pp. 107–108). On Luther's connection with medieval mysticism, see Bengt Hoffmann: *Luther and the Mystics,* Minneapolis, 1976; on Rhineland mysticism generally, James M. Clark: *The Great German Mystics,* Oxford, 1949.

41. Ch. 3, 28, p. 530.

42. Ch. 5, 1, p. 560.

43. Ch. 5, 13, p. 574.

44. Ch. 4, 8, p. 539.

45. On Melanchthon (1497–1560) see Clyde L. Manschreck, *op. cit.*; Robert Stupperich: *Melanchthon,* Philadelphia, 1960.

46. Dillenberger, *op. cit.*, pp. 502–503.

47. "The Creator, the Perfect, cannot be comprehended, known, and described in the same manner by creatures, on account of their creatureliness. The Perfect must consequently be nameless because it is not any created thing" (*Theologia Germanica*, Ch. 1, *op. cit.*, p. 60). On Eckhart, see James M. Clark: *Meister Eckhart. An Introduction to the Study of His Works with an Anthology of His Sermons*, London, 1957; Jeanne Lancelot-Hustache: *Master Eckhart and the Rhineland Mystics*, New York, 1957.

48. The *Commentary on Galatians*, 1535, is in W.A., Vol. 40, I and 40, II. I will indicate the volume before the page. This quotation, ch. 3, 10, Vol. I, p. 410.

49. Ch. 2, 14, Vol. I, p. 207.

50. Ch. 1, 33, Vol. I, p. 77.

51. Ch. 3, 6, Vol. I, p. 360.

52. Ch. 3, 6, Vol. I, p. 371.

53. See ch. 3, 10, Vol. I, p. 410.

54. Ch. 3, 19, Vol. I, p. 417.

55. Ch. 3, 10, Vol. I, p. 417.

56. Ch. 3, 10, Vol. I, p. 410.

57. Ch. 4, 24, Vol. I, p. 657.

58. Ch. 4, 8, I, p. 610.

59. Ch. 4, 19, I, p. 650.

60. *La Théologie parmi les sciences humaines*, pp. 36–39.

61. Ch. 2, 16, I, p. 218.

62. Ch. 2, 20, I, pp. 292–293.

63. Ch. 2, 6, I, p. 182.

64. Ch. 3, 2; I, p. 423.

65. Ch. 5, 9; II, p. 48.

66. Ch. 5, 10; II, p. 49.

67. Ch. 5, 9; II, p. 48.

68. Ch. 5, 9; II, p. 47.

69. The Reformed tradition will wish to restore *caritas* to a central place, especially under the influence of Heinrich Bullinger (1504–1575), the successor of Zwingli in Zurich; see J. Wayne Baker: *Heinrich Bullinger and the Covenant: The Other Reformed Tradition*, Athens, Ohio, 1980.

70. Ch. 6, 2; II, p. 144.

71. Ch. 3, 10; I, p. 423.

72. Ch. 5, 5; II, p. 23.

73. Ch. 5, 5; II, p. 24.

74. Ch. 5, 5; II, p. 24.

75. Ch. 5, 5; II, p. 25.

76. Ch. 5, 5; II, p. 25.
77. Ch. 5, 5; II, pp. 26–27.
78. Ch. 5, 5; II, p. 28.
79. Ch. 5, 5; II, p. 24.
80. Ch. 3, 10; I, p. 402.
81. Ch. 3, 10; I, p. 407.
82. Ch. 3, 10; I, p. 408.
83. Ch. 3, 10; I, p. 410.
84. Ch. 3, 6; I, p. 364.
85. Ch. 3, 6; I, pp. 366–367.
86. Ch. 16; I, p. 220.
87. On the bondage of the will, see Harry McSorley: *Luther: Right or Wrong?* New York, 1969.
88. Ch. 2, 16; I, pp. 228–229.
89. Calvin's three uses of the Law are the following: (1) a convincing and condemning function regarding one's unrighteousness (*Inst,* II, ch. 7, n. 6); (2) a liberating function in regard to evil, this liberation resulting from fear of punishment (n. 10); (3) an educative function among the faithful, who, through knowledge of the Law, come to know "better and with more certitude to understand the will of God to which they aspire" (n. 12). This would be the main function of the Law. The Lutheran *Formula of Concord* (1580) formulates the three uses of the Law differently: (1) to maintain external discipline among the wicked, (2) to lead the faithful people to confess their sins, (3) to give the faithful a rule of life (*Epitome,* VI; this is further explained in *Solida declaratio,* VI). Calvin's first and second uses correspond to the second of the *Formula;* his third is expressed more spiritually. Through the external use of the Law (1) and the notion of rule for the faithful (3), the Lutheran discussions introduced a more legalistic dimension than Calvin allowed for.
90. *Institutes,* II, ch. 8, n. 5. Note Calvin's balanced formulation: *Fides ergo sola est quae justificat; fides tamen quae justificat non est sola* (It is faith alone which justifies; but the faith which justifies is not alone), in *Acta synodi Tridentinae cum antidoto* (*Opera,* Vol. 7, 1868, col. 477).
91. *Institutes,* II, ch. 11, n. 5. For a modern treatment of justification in the Calvinist tradition, see G. C. Berkouwer: *Faith and Justification,* Grand Rapids, 1954. Berkouwer's method, however, gives more importance to the Calvinist confessions and the Synod of Dort than to the more nuanced theology of Calvin; it also frequently proceeds by way of contrast with "Rome," but Roman Catholic doctrine is commonly misunderstood. Berkouwer sums up his view with these words: "justification on the ground of nothing . . . " (p. 89). Calvin would have been astonished!

92. *Institutes,* II, ch. 11, n. 1.

93. Richard Hooker: *A Learned Discourse of Justification,* n. 3, in *The Laws of Ecclesiastical Polity,* Vol. I, London, 1954, p. 17.

94. *Op. cit.,* n. 21, p. 37.

95. The other delegates of the Church of England were G. Carlton, bishop of Llandaff, J. Davenant, S. Ward, and W. Balcanquall; the decrees of Dort are in Philip Schaff: *The Creeds of Christendom,* Vol. III, New York, 1877, pp. 500–597. On the impact of justification by faith in the English Reformation, see David B. Knox: *The Doctrine of Faith in the Reign of Henry VIII,* London, 1961; William A. Clebsch: *England's Earliest Protestants, 1520–1535,* New Haven, 1964.

Chapter IV

1. The Colloquy of Regensburg (April–July 1541) sought for a compromise between Luther and the Catholic theologians on the main points in dispute. The Lutheran delegation was headed by Melanchthon (Luther did not attend); the Catholic delegation was led by the Venetian diplomat and lay cardinal, Gasparo Contarini (1483–1542), who was himself, through his spiritual experience, convinced that the doctrine of justification by faith was correct. In regard to justification, the *Regensburg Book,* containing the Colloquy's agreement, opted for a doctrine of double justice. On Contarini, see Orestes Ferrara: *Gasparo Contarini et ses missions,* Paris, 1956; on the Regensburg Colloquy: Walter von Lowenich: *Duplex Justitia. Luthers Stellung zu einer Unionsformel des 16. Jahrhunderts,* Wiesbaden, 1972; Heiko Oberman: *Werden und Wertung der Reformation,* pp. 109–113; on Luther's own use of the concept of double justice: Daniel Olivier: *Les deux sermons sur la double et la triple justice* (*Oecumenica,* 3, 1968, pp. 39–69).

2. On the history of the Council of Trent as regards justification, see Hubert Jedin: *Geschichte des Konzils von Trient,* Vol. 2, Freiburg, 1957, pp. 139–268; Eduard Stakemeier: *Glaube und Rechtfertigung. Das Mysterium der christlichen Rechtfertigung aus dem Glauben dargestellt nach der Verhandlungen und Lehrbestimmungen des Konzils von Trient,* Freiburg, 1937; Henri Rondet: *The Grace of Christ. A Brief History of the Theology of Grace,* New York, 1967. Ferdinand Cavallera's important articles on the sixth session of the Council have not been put in book form: *La session VI du concile de Trente* (*Bulletin de littérature écclésiastique,* Toulouse, 1943, pp. 229–238; 1944, pp. 220–231; 1945, pp. 54–64; 1946, pp. 103–112; *Le Décret du concile de Trente sur la justification,* 1948, pp. 21–31; 1950, pp. 65–76 and 146–168; *La Session VI du concile de Trente. Foi et justification,* 1952, pp. 99–108. See also Hefele-Leclercq: *Histoire des Conciles,* Vol. 9, Paris, 1930, pp. 303–357.

3. D.S., n. 1256.

4. D.S., n. 1529.

5. This notion was based on an analogy between faith as human trust in witnesses, and faith as acceptance of the apostles' testimony concerning Christ and revelation; ecclesiastical faith, or trust in the Church's testimony and teaching, was seen as intermediate between those two. One finds such a theology in Henry Holden: *Analysis divinae fidei,* 1652; see Tavard: *The Seventeenth-Century Tradition. A Study in Recusant Thought.* Leide, 1978, pp. 180–196. Similar distinctions have persisted into the twentieth century in some schools of Catholic theology.

6. *Commentary on Galatians,* ch. 4, 5 (W.A., Vol. 2, p. 536).

7. D.S., n. 1529.

8. D.S., n. 1530.

9. D.S., n. 1531.

10. D.S., n. 1533.

11. D.S., n. 1526.

12. D.S., n. 1547.

13. D.S., n. 1532.

14. The conciliar decree of Trent includes thirty-three canons, containing anathemas against the proponents of various positions underscored in these canons. While neither Luther nor Calvin is named, it is easy to see that the Council had the two reformers primarily in mind. However, two points should be made. First, each canon needs to be compared to the authentic doctrines of the Reformation, so that the question may be answered: Did the Council really know the true doctrine of the reformers, as these understood it? Second, the canons are more polemically oriented than the expository part of the decree; in good methodology, the doctrine of the Council is to be found in this exposition, not in the canons, which only illustrate the application of this doctrine to some polemical points of Reformation teaching, as these were understood at the Council. There is no *a priori* guarantee that the reformers taught what is condemned there.

15. On the controversy *de auxiliis,* see the article *Grace,* by J. Van der Meersch, in D.T.C., Vol. VI, nn. 1554–1687, especially 1664–1684; Henri Rondet: *op. cit.,* 313–339; on the broad background of the question, see Henri de Lubac: *The Mystery of the Supernatural,* New York, 1967; *Augustinianism and Modern Theology,* London, 1969.

16. D.S., 2001–2007 (the five propositions); 2600–2700 (Pistoia). On Jansenism, see Louis Cognet: *Le Jansénisme,* Paris, 1961; Henri Rondet, *op. cit.,* pp. 340–362; René Taveneaux: *Le Catholicisme dans la France classique, 1610–1715,* 2 vols., Paris, 1980.

17. See the relevant chapters in my study, *La Tradition au XVIIe siècle en France et en Angleterre,* Paris, 1969.

18. My references will be to the English translation, which I have modified in places: Sr. Generosa Callahan, ed.: *The Dogma of Grace,* San Antonio, 1979, p. 3. On Moye, see Sr. Generosa Callahan: *The Life of Blessed John Martin Moye,* Milwaukee, 1964; Georges Tavard: *L'Expérience de Jean-Martin Moye,* 1730–1793, Paris, 1978.

19. *Ibid.,* 1978, p. 4.

20. *Ibid.,* p. 94.

21. *Ibid.,* p. 96.

22. *Ibid.,* p. 98. The main theological sources of Moye's theology were Pierre Collet (1693–1770), whose manuals were studied at St. Simon Seminary, Metz, which Moye attended, and Honoré Tournély (1658–1729), a theologian from the Sorbonne who was famous in his time; see *L'Expérience* . . . ., pp. 84–85.

23. *Ibid.,* p. 101.

24. *Ibid.,* p. 86.

25. *Ibid.,* p. 84.

26. *Ibid.,* p. 36.

27. *Ibid.,* pp. 40–42.

28. *Ibid.,* pp. 86–87.

29. *Ibid.,* p. 97.

30. *Ibid.,* p. 102; Moye in fact had no direct knowledge of the doctrines of the reformers.

31. *Ibid.,* p. 78.

32. *Ibid.,* p. 63.

33. John Wesley: *A Plain Account of Christian Perfection,* London, 1968, p. 61. This expression is found in Moye's writings; see *L'Expérience* . . . , pp. 66–67; its source is *The Imitation of Christ,* III, ch. 4; on Moye and the *Imitation,* see *op. cit.,* pp. 92–93.

34. See Maximin Piette: *John Wesley in the Evolution of Protestantism,* New York, 1937.

35. On the *Homilies,* see below.

36. See Frank Baker: *John Wesley and the Church of England,* Nashville, 1970; on the doctrine of justification, see William Cannon: *The Theology of John Wesley, with Special Reference to the Doctrine of Justification,* New York, 1946; Charles Koerber: *The Theology of Conversion according to John Wesley,* New York, 1967. Wesley shows his own concern about justification by publishing a selection of passages on the topic from the great Puritan divine, Richard Baxter (1615–1691): *An Extract from Mr. Richard*

Baxter's Aphorisms of Justification; and from the Anglican John Goodwin (c. 1594–1665): *A Treatise on Justification extracted from Mr. John Goodwin.*

37. Text in Albert Outler, ed.: *John Wesley,* New York, 1964, p. 66.

38. Ditto, respectively pp. 62–63, 64, 65.

39. Baker, *op. cit.,* p. 9.

40. Article XI—adopted, among the thirty-nine Articles of the Church of England, in 1562—runs as follows: *"Of the Justification of Man.* We are accounted righteous before God, only for the merit of our Lord and Saviour Jesus Christ by Faith, and not for our own works and deservings. Wherefore, that we are justified by Faith only, is a wholesome Doctrine, and very full of comfort, as more largely is expressed in the Homily of Justification." This article was kept by Wesley as Article IX of the Methodist associations without the reference to the *Homilies.*

41. Outler, *op. cit.,* p. 127.

42. *The Works of John Wesley,* Grand Rapids, 1958, Vol. 5, p. 7. This sermon, entitled, "Salvation through faith," was preached on June 11, and again on June 18, 1738.

43. Piette, *op. cit.,* p. 312. In his *Faith Seeking Understanding,* Durham, N.C., 1981. pp. 51–74, Robert E. Cushman argues that Wesley's understanding of justification was that of the reformers, rediscovered by Wesley against the deistic and Pelagian positions of most Anglicans in the eighteenth century. But this is to forget the significant differences which did exist between Luther and Calvin on the question, and to overlook Wesley's critique of Luther on the question of Law and Gospel.

44. Piette, *op. cit.,* p. 329.

45. *The Journal of John Wesley,* London, 1938, Vol. II, p. 315.

46. *A Plain Account* . . . , p. 13.

47. *Journal,* Vol. II, p. 467.

48. Outler, *op. cit.,* p. 137.

49. *Ibid.*

50. Outler, *op. cit.,* p. 205.

51. Piette, *op. cit.,* p. 326.

52. Outler, *op. cit.,* p. 277.

53. *Journal,* Vol. II, p. 329.

54. Outler, *op. cit.,* p. 201.

55. *Ibid.,* p. 274.

56. *Ibid.,* p. 267.

57. *Ibid.,* p. 140.

58. Piette, *op. cit.,* p. 439.

59. *Ibid.,* p. 442.

60. *A Plain Account* . . . , p. 41.

61. Outler, *op. cit.,* p. 234. On quietism, see Ronald Knox: *Enthusiasm,* Oxford, 1950, pp. 260–318 (in general), 288–318 (in Spain), 318–355 (in France), 389–421 (among the Moravians). Knox's pages on Wesley (422–548) are worth reading, despite his usual reliance on second- or third-hand material.

62. *A Plain Account* . . . , pp. 70–71.

63. *Ibid.,* p. 71.

64. John Henry Newman: *Lectures on the Doctrine of Justification,* 8th impr., London, 1900, p. ix.

65. P. 348. Albert Pighi (c. 1490–1542), a Louvain theologian, held for a moderate doctrine of double righteousness; Cornelio Musso (1511–1574), bishop of Bitonto during the Council of Trent, was closely connected with the early text of the Tridentine decree; see A. Mobilia: *Cornelio Musso e la prima forma del decreto sulla giustificazione,* Naples, 1960.

66. *Ibid.,* p. 358.

67. *Ibid.,* pp. 348–349. *The Roman Catechism,* also known as the *Catechism of the Council of Trent,* or the *Catechism of Pius V,* written at the request of the Council of Trent, was published in 1566, as a model for future national or regional catechisms. Rather than what is conventionally called a catechism, however, it is a solid piece of theological synthesis, in the spirit of the Tridentine Council.

68. *Ibid.,* p. 343.

69. *Ibid.,* p. 278.

70. *Ibid.,* p. ix.

Chapter V

1. *Responsio ad Lutherum* (*Complete Works of St. Thomas More,* Vol. 5, New Haven, Conn., 1969, p. 268).

2. Quoted in Philipp Schäfer: *Die Einheit der Kirche in der Katholischen Theologie der Aufklarung,* Georg Schwaiger, ed.: *Zwischen Polemik und Irenik. Untersuchungen zum Verhaltnis der Konfessionen in spaten 18. und fruhen 19. Jahrhundert,* Göttingen, 1977, p. 41.

3. Matthias Scheeben: *Handbuch der katholischen Dogmatik,* Vol. 4, part 1, Freiburg, 1898, pp. 15–16.

4. D.S., nn. 3008–3010, 3013. Vatican I issued two doctrinal constitutions: *Dei Filius,* on the Christian faith, and *Pastor aeternus,* on papal authority. More attention has been paid to the latter on account of the controversial nature of its definition of papal infallibility. Information on the background of *Dei Filius* may be found in Theodor Granderath: *Geschichte des Vatikanisches Konzils,* Vol. II, Freiburg, 1903, pp. 79–133, 361–508; E.

Cuthbert Butler: *The Vatican Council, 1869–1870,* Westminster, Md., 1962, pp. 235–247; Henri Rondet: *Vatican I,* Paris, 1962, pp. 95–115; James Hennesey: *The First Council of the Vatican. The American Experience,* New York, 1963, pp. 130–171; Roger Aubert: *Vatican I,* Paris, 1964, pp. 182–194. Vatican I was concerned about the credibility of faith (can one show that reasonable assent may be given to the Christian faith?) and its credentity (can one show that total assent should be given to the Christian faith?). Such problems have had, in fact, excessive importance in Catholic apologetics during the nineteenth and twentieth centuries; see Avery Dulles: *A History of Apologetics,* New York, 1971. Some aspects of this apologetics were anticipated in English Recusant theology; see Tavard: *The Seventeenth-Century Tradition. A Study in Recusant Thought,* Leide, 1978, pp. 180–196. Nonetheless, *Dei Filius* reflected also the theology of its chief redactor, Cardinal Victor Dechamps (1861–1939), and the "method of immanence"; see Raymond Saint-Jean: *L'Apologétique Philosophique: Blondel, 1893–1913,* Paris, 1966, pp. 137–155. Most of the principles later expounded at length by Karl Rahner and embodied in his "transcendental method" are already fully developed in Blondel's analysis of action.

5. D.S., nn. 3008, 3010.

6. D.S., n. 3010.

7. D.S., n. 3010.

8. D.S., n. 3012.

9. D.S., n. 3019.

10. D.S., nn. 2775–2786.

11. D.S., n. 3008.

12. See Avery Dulles, *op. cit.,* pp. 202–221.

13. Josef Lortz: *Die Reformation in Deutschland,* 2 vols., Freiburg, 1939–1940. On the assumed Pelagianism of the Nominalists, see above, Chapter II, note 12.

14. Among authors who endorsed Lortz's interpretations, one may mention Adolf Stakemeir: *Das Konzil von Trient Über die Heilsgewissheit,* Heidelberg, 1947; William van de Pol: *Das reformatorische Christentum,* Zurich, 1956, pp. 381–445; Otto Pesch's exhaustive study was published later: *Die Theologie der Rechtfertigung bei Martin Luther und Thomas von Aquin,* Mainz, 1967.

15. *Rechtfertigung. Die Lehre Karl Barths und eine katholische Besinnung,* Einsiedeln, 1957; English tr., *Justification. The Doctrine of Karl Barth and a Catholic Reflection,* New York, 1964. This important book was first presented to the American public by myself: *Catholic Views on Karl Barth* (*Christian Century,* February 1959, pp. 132–133).

16. *Justification,* p. 69.

17. *Ibid.,* p. 236.

18. *Ibid.,* p. 282.

19. *Ibid.,* p. 284.

20. Pesch, *Twenty Years* . . . , p. 10. I draw on this essay in the next few pages.

21. *Ibid.,* p. 13.

22. English tr.: *The Grace of Christ,* Westminster, Md., 1966. See pp. 275–289. Edward Yarnold: *The Second Gift. A Study of Grace,* London, 1974, has only a few allusions to Luther. See H.J. Kouvenhoven: *Simul justus et Peccator in de nieuwe roomskatholicke theologie,* Delft, 1969; Martin Bogdahn: *Die Rechtfertigungslehre Luthers in Urteil der neueren katholischem Theologie,* Göttingen, 1971.

23. Paris, 1954; English tr.: *The Spirit and Forms of Protestantism,* Westminster, Md., 1956.

24. *Ibid.,* p. 61; English tr., p. 58.

25. *Le Protestantisme,* Paris, 1958, pp. 28–29; English tr., *Protestantism,* New York, 1959, pp. 27–29. Note the translator's bias: where the French text said *pas hétérodoxe* (not heterodox), she wrote, "not so objectionable." The reference to Calvin in the quotation is to *Institutes,* III, ch. 19, n. 9.

26. *Questions of Controversial Theology on Justification* (*Theological Investigations,* Vol. IV, Baltimore, 1966, p. 198).

27. *Justified and Sinner at the Same Time* (*op. cit.,* Vol. VI, 1969, p. 221).

28. *Ibid.,* pp. 219–220.

29. *Ibid.,* p. 223.

30. *Ibid.*

31. *Ibid.,* pp. 227–228.

32. *Ibid.,* p. 229.

33. *Ibid.*

34. E.g., Harry McSorley, *op. cit.*; Stephanus Pfürtner: *Luther und Thomas in Gespraech. Unser Heilzwischen Gewissheit und Gefardung,* Heidelberg, 1961; Wolfgang Stein: *Das kirchlische Amt bei Luther,* Wiesbaden, 1974; Daniel Oliver: *La Foi de Luther,* Paris, 1979.

35. Tavard, ed.: *Dogmatic Constitution on Divine Revelation,* New York, 1966, p. 60.

36. *Ibid.,* p. 25.

37. Edward Yarnold, *op. cit.,* p. 90.

38. Hans Urs von Balthasar: *Adrienne von Speyr et sa mission théologique,* Paris, 1976, p. 100.

39. Jean-Martin Moye, quoted in Tavard: *L'Expérience de Jean-Martin Moye. Mystique et mission,* Paris, 1978, p. 146.

40. Maurice Blondel: *Letter on Apologetics and History and Dogma,* New York, 1964, p. 225; Paul Tillich: *Systematic Theology,* Vol. I, Chicago, 1951, p. 84. Blondel is openly opposed to "extrinsicism" in regard to grace and revelation; yet he also maintains what he calls "l'hétéronomie de la grâce" (*La Notion et le rôle du miracle,* in *Annales de Philosophie Chrétienne,* 1907, p. 345).

41. *Philosophical Grammar,* Berkeley, 1978, p. 267.

42. See *Lutherans and Catholics in Dialogue,* I–III, Minneapolis, 1974 (on the Nicene Creed, baptism, the Eucharist); IV, 1979 (on ministry); V, 1974 (on papal primacy); VI, 1980 (on teaching authority and infallibility). For a general introduction, see Joseph A. Burgess and George H. Tavard: *Studies for Lutheran-Catholic Dialogue,* Minneapolis, 1980.

43. *Dei Verbum,* n. 10, *op. cit.,* p. 67.

Conclusion

1. See *Justification Today. Studies and Reports* (*Lutheran World,* supplement to No. 1, 1965); *A Study Document on Justification,* National Lutheran Council, N.Y., 1966.

2. *Report of the Joint Lutheran/Roman Catholic Study Commission on "The Gospel and the Church,"* n. 26 (*Lutheran World,* Vol. XIX, n.3, 1972, p. 5).

3. *Lutheran-Episcopal Dialogue. Report and Recommendations,* Cincinnati, 1981, p. 23.

4. Enrico Di Negri: *La Teologia di Lutero,* Florence, 1967, p. 301.

5. *Istituto Paolo VI. Notiziario n. 3,* Brescia, May 1981, p. 33. This is taken from a series of essays entitled, *La Preghiera dell'Anima,* originally published in *Studium* (Journal of the Italian Catholic University Federation) from January to June 1930.

INDEX

Abelard, Peter, 35f
Alberto Pio, 59
Alexander of Hales, 37
Andrew de Vega, 25f
asceticism, 20, 23, 81f

Banez, Dominic, 80
baptism, 10, 20
Barth, Karl, 100f
Biel, Gabriel, 46f
Blondel, Maurice, 109
Boniface II, Pope, 24
Bossuet, 81
Bouyer, Louis, 102f
Bradwardine, Thomas, 46
Bucer, Martin, 93f

Caesarius of Arles, 24
Calvin, Jean, 58, 68f, 71, 86, 93
Charles the Bald, King, 27
Church of England, 85
conversion, 2f, 8, 14, 18, 20, 23f, 34, 75
Council of Carthage (418), 23, 28
Council of Orange II (529), 24, 42, 73ff, 99, 106f
Council of Sens (1140), 35f
Council of the Vatican I, 96–99, 106, 113
Council of the Vatican II, 2, 106f

Council of Trent, 68–80, 84, 93, 99ff
Cranmer, Thomas, 68, 86

Di Negri, Henrico, 113
Duns Scotus, John, 43–47, 74

Eckhart, 59
ecumenical dialogues, 1f, 110ff
Erasmus, 59, 67

facienti quod in se est . . . 36f, 40f, 44, 47f, 57f, 63, 75, 89, 91
faith, 19, 23f, 31f, 60, 64f, 71ff, 77ff, 84, 88f, 97ff, 106f
faith alone, 20, 51ff, 59, 68ff, 106f
Faustus of Riez, 23
Fénelon, 81
forensic justice, 31, 65f
free will, 21, 27f, 33f, 44, 67, 92

Gerhard, 93
Gerson, Jean, 46
Gilbert Porretanus, 36
good works, 20–23, 86f
Gospel, 6, 12, 16, 24, 52–61, 86, 91, 97, 109
Gottschalk, 25–28
grace, 2, 19, 25, 30–37, 75, 79, 81–84, 99
Gregory of Rimini, 46f